Kingsna...

by Robert Applegate

Professional Breeders Series®

© 2007 by ECO Herpetological Publishing & Distribution.

ISBN 978-0-9788979-0-1

No part of this book may be reproduced or utilized in any form or by any means, electronic or mechanical, including photocopying, recording, or by any information storage or retrieval systems, without permission in writing from the publisher.

Copies available from:

ECO Herpetological Publishing & Distribution
915 Seymour Ave. Lansing, MI 48906 USA
telephone: 517.487.5595   fax: 517.371.2709
email: ecoorders@hotmail.com   website: http://www.reptileshirts.com

T-Rex Products, Inc.   LIVING ART publishing
http://t-rexproducts.com   http://www.livingartpublishing.com

Zoo Book Sales   APPLEGATE REPTILES
http://www.zoobooksales.com   http://www.applegatereptiles.com

Design and layout by Russ Gurley.
Cover design by Rafael Porrata.

Printed in China.

Front Cover: A handsome Arizona Mountain Kingsnake. Photo by Don Soderberg.
Back Cover: A vanishing pattern hypomelanistic Honduran Milksnake. Photo by Terry Dunham.

I dedicate this book to my "Oregon Farm Girl", wife, and best friend, Marilee J. Applegate, who brought a sense of appreciation and completion to my life.

Acknowledgements. So who do I thank? That is a tough one! I have picked up bits and pieces of information my entire life from many people I have met. I am fortunate enough to travel around and have people share information with me, so if I have ever met you, attended your lecture, read your article or book, or otherwise communicated with you, there is probably a small bit of you in this book, and I thank you.

There are certain people deserving special mention, several of which are listed here. Many inadvertently left out. Bob and Sheri Ashley for promising me fame and fortune for completing this project, my editor Russ Gurley (Here I am supposed to take the blame for any errors, but only content errors are mine, editing errors, if any, are his! That's why he gets the big bucks), Ed Bradley, Pat Russnell, Alan Botterman (It's amazing what you learn hanging around the T-Rex folks in product development), Ron and Mary Huffaker, Dr. Rosanne Brown, William Moran, Jeff Lemm, Richard Sturm, Rick and Becky Trenny, Michael and "Becca" Clarkson, Dr. Lee Grismer, Phillipe DeVosjoli, Monty Krizan, Paul Lynum, Bill Love, all that submitted photos for the book, accepted for print or not, and especially you, the reader. You hold the future of herpetoculture in your destiny. Get out there and make us old timers proud. Herpetoculture really got its start in the 1970s and in the last 30 some years we have made amazing strides. But I feel after the next 30 years pass (I hope I am there) we will look back on today as a primitive time in the development. And lastly, a plea! Can't we all get along? Imagine what we could accomplish if the scientists and the private herpeticulturists would cooperate with each other!

TABLE OF CONTENTS

INTRODUCTION	1
Chapter ONE: General Information . .	5
Chapter TWO: Housing and Maintenance.. .	14
Chapter THREE: Your Pet Kingsnake . .	29
Chapter FOUR: Feeding	36
Chapter FIVE: Breeding Kingsnakes. . .	49
Chapter SIX: Diseases and Disorders . .	65
Final Comments	70
Sinaloan Mountain Kingsnake . . .	73
PHOTO GALLERY	77
SUGGESTED READING	89

INTRODUCTION

A beautiful Gray-banded Kingsnake. *Lampropeltis alterna.* Photo by Bill Love.

As a group, kingsnakes are among the most popular snakes currently kept by reptile enthusiasts. As a result, only a few kingsnakes are still collected in some numbers from the wild; most are captive-bred and have become increasingly available in the general pet trade.

There are now nine recognized species of kingsnakes. The nine species are (latin name/common name) *Lampropeltis alterna* - Texas Gray-banded Kingsnake, *L. calligaster* - Prairie Kingsnake, *L. getula* - Common Kingsnake, *L. mexicana* - Mexican Gray-banded Kingsnake AKA San Luis Potosi Kingsnake, *L. pyromelana* - Arizona Mountain Kingsnake, *L. ruthveni* - Ruthvens Kingsnake, *L. triangulum* - Milksnake (Yes, milksnakes are kingsnakes), *L. webbi* - Sinaloan Mountain Kingsnake (You will be introduced to this later in the book), and *L. zonata* - California Mountain Kingsnake

All the kingsnakes are very "convenient" to keep in captivity. Their small size, simple cage requirements, easily supplied diet (for most species), adaptability to life in captivity, and great beauty have made

Vanishing pattern hypomelanistic Honduran Milksnake. Photo by Terry Dunham.

them popular with beginning hobbyists as well as with more advanced herpetoculturists. Their bright, sharply contrasting colors (red/orange, black, and white/yellow bands circle the body in many of the kingsnakes) and crisp patterns invariably tend to elicit "Oh!" and "Ah!" exclamations from non-reptile enthusiasts as well.

As of 1990 Markel recognized eight species of kingsnake. In 2000 a new species of kingsnake was collected in Mexico. This new species (*Lampropeltis webbi*) was described for science in "Journal of Herpetology" Vol. 39 in 2005 by Drs. Bryson, Jr, Dixon, and Lazcano, and named in honor of Dr. Robert Webb for his contributions to the research on herpetofauna of northwestern Mexico. The other eight species are (Latin name/Common name) - *Lampropeltis alterna* (Texas Gray-banded Kingsnake), *Lampropeltis calligaster* (Prairie Kingsnake), *Lampropeltis getula* (Common Kingsnake), *Lampropeltis mexicana* (Mexican Gray-banded Kingsnake/San Luis Potosi Kingsnake), *Lampropeltis pyromelana* (Arizona Mountain Kingsnake), *Lampropeltis ruthveni* (Ruthven's Kingsnake), *Lampropeltis triangulum* (Milksnake), *and Lampropeltis zonata* (California Mountain Kingsnake). Six of the nine species of kingsnakes have subspecies. The remaining three do not.

Three distinct color patterns of *Lampropeltis mexicana thayeri* exist. All three of these snakes came from the same clutch. Photo by Bob Applegate.

As of 1988, Williams recognized 25 subspecies of the milk snake *Lampropeltis triangulum*. Some of the other species have a lesser number of subspecies described. These numbers may ultimately vary depending on the particular taxonomic trend governing the field of herpetology at a particular point in time. Many of these subspecies have been successfully reproduced in captivity for many generations and their maintenance has become almost a recipe. On the other hand, subspecies recently discovered or which are very rare in collections, and new color variations which are occasionally turning up, need much more work before their "recipe" for captive care and breeding can be published.

My goal with this book is to provide you with essential information for the long-term care and maintenance of this beautiful and variable genus of snake. I have chosen to present this in an informal manner, writing as if we were in the same room carrying on a conversation. Most of what is contained in this book are my personal opinions, based on many years of my own experience and the shared knowledge of others.

An additional goal, should you choose to be a part of this program, is to provide you with the information needed to reproduce the chosen species and subspecies in captivity and provide additional specimens

A double-striped California Kingsnake, Lampropeltis getula californiae. Photo by Don Shores.

for the public, thereby reducing the need and demand to collect large numbers of additional wild specimens. Besides establishing alternate populations of possibly uncommon or rare species, you will also benefit from being able to enhance your personal income. I am a strong advocate of "Conservation Through Captive Propagation."

Chapter ONE: General Information

Lampropeltis zonata agalma. Photo by Bob Applegate.

WHAT'S IN A NAME?

Common Name

Kingsnake? Why king? My best guess is they were called kingsnakes because of their ability to kill and eat venomous snakes. Another good guess, because they eat almost any other animal small enough to be swallowed whole. They are powerful constrictors, minature versions of the giant pythons. Perfect killing machines. What could be better than a living mouse trap that can crawl down the mouse hole, and kill and eat the entire mouse family without poisoning the environment with toxins? Milk snakes? (Yes milksnakes are one of the nine species of kingsnakes) .They don't really milk cows, do they? Rest assured, milk snakes do NOT milk cows. Long before our time some dairyman with a sense of humor must have noticed a milk snake or two in his barn. When he didn't get the desired quantity of milk from his cow(s) he may have remarked that the milk snakes must have sucked the cows dry the night before. In spite of their name, the hard working milk snakes had simply been drawn to the barn while seeking their normal dinner of mice. Even if it could suck milk, an amount equivalent to the body volume of a milk snake would hardly be missed from a milk-producing cow. I have been assured by those who know, that a cow wouldn't stand still while six rows of needle-sharp teeth were clamped on her teat.

Scientific Name

Kingsnakes are members of the large snake family Colubridae and belong to the genus *Lampropeltis*. They are divided into the nine species of kingsnakes. Many of the species (six of nine) are further divided into subspecies. This can get a bit confusing to some, so I like to use a car analogy. Kingsnake (*Lampropeltis*) = Fords, species=models (T-Bird, Pickup, Sedan), and subspecies= different colors. So all T-Birds are Fords, but all Fords are not T-Birds. All Milksnakes are kingsnakes, but all kingsnakes are not milksnakes. The taxonomy involved in determining which species/subspecies a snake should be assigned to is way beyond the scope of this book. But once the true herpetologists (people with scientific training and a high tolerance for boredom, spending many hours counting scales soaked in smelly preservatives) assign them to a species and subspecies , that is where we come into the picture to possess and properly care for the snake in captivity. That would make us herpetoculturists, not herpetologists. You could be both, but there is certainly a difference. Many herpetologists never touch a living reptile. Some of the species of kingsnakes have a few subspecies, while the milksnake has many. In his monograph, Williams (1988) recognizes 25 subspecies of the milk snake *Lampropeltis triangulum*. Since then at least one more milksnake subspecies has been described.

The current trend in herpetoculture is to refer to various kingsnakes using both common and scientific names though the general use of scientific names is becoming increasingly widespread usually at the subspecific level when referring to kingsnakes. For example, herpetoculturists in the course of their conversations will commonly use "hondurensis" or "campbelli" or "annulata" or knoblocki or pyro (short for *pyromelana*) to refer to those respective kingsnake subspecies.

Lampropeltis getula conjuncta. Photo by Michael Clarkson and Jeff Mintz.

Scientific names are used because they standardize, eliminate confusion, and insure one common international language in biological classification and identification. Common names are considered to be too localized in nature and their variation would confuse international communications. As an example, lets say you are in England and one of your friends in Italy wants to send you a "Blacksnake". You think he is talking about the Black Racer from the USA, a harmless snake, but you receive a Blacksnake from Australia, a venomous relative of the cobra, oops!! If you were given the scientific name this error would not be made. Latin and Greek are the chosen languages for scientific names. The standard format for scientific names is as follows: first, the genus, then the species. For example, all milksnakes belong to the genus *Lampropeltis* and the species *triangulum*. If there is more than one subspecies, the species name is repeated again as the subspecific name of the originally described animal for the species. In all other subsequently described subspecies, the subspecific name will be different although the genus and species will remain the same as in the originally described species name. For example, when originally described (for simplicity I am disregarding previously used and revised names) the Eastern Milksnake was known as *Lampropeltis triangulum*. That was it, two names.

The original binomial system proposed by Carl Linnaeus in the 1700's to describe all living things. Later many other variations or subspecies of milk snake were discovered. For example, the Pueblan Milksnake, which was named after J. Campbell, the man who brought it back to science, was described as *Lampropeltis triangulum campbelli*. The eastern milk snake, to distinguish it from the other triangulum subspecies, had its scientific name repeated at the subspecific level and became *Lampropeltis triangulum triangulum*.

If you are wondering who gives the snakes these names, it is the person who "describes for science" the animal who gets to assign the name and submit it for acceptance to a board of peers. Some snake names mean nothing (that we can figure out), most are something of a description. For instance "Lampropeltis"-the genus referring to kingsnakes-was derived from lampros which is Greek for shining, beautiful, and pelte from the Greek meaning small shield. Roughly translated, Lampropeltis could mean small beautiful shield, presumably referring to the shiny scales of the kingsnake.

Taxonomy is a field which is continually updated as new information is acquired on the relationships between various species and

The originally described Mexican Gray-banded Kingsnakes AKA San Luis Potosi Kingsnake, *Lampropeltis mexicana mexicana*. Photo by Bob Applegate.

Typical habitat for Mexican Gray-banded Kingsnakes/San Luis Potosi Kingsnake *Lampropeltis mexicana mexicana* in San Luis Potosi, Mexico. Photo by Bob Applegate.

subspecies. There are roughly speaking, two trends of thought in taxonomy. The "splitters" are the taxonomists who will name a new species or subspecies on the slightest differences. The taxonomic "lumpers" want fewer groups and want to consolidate the existing ones. The ultimate "lumper" would consider all 25+ subspecies of the milk snake color or geographic variations that should all be called *Lampropeltis triangulum* with no subspecies. As a rule, herpetoculturists place a considerable emphasis on geographical variants and would probably prefer a standardization of a language that allows for a descriptive isolation of these variants.

Tricolors

Tricolors? This is a term most often used by herpetoculturists to generally describe many kingsnakes and most milk snakes with the ringed three-color pattern. There are many venomous and other non-venomous species of snakes that are also tricolored but most are not popular either because they are dangerous or because of their difficult captive requirements.

Distribution

The kingsnake (*Lampropeltis*) is an American species found from southeastern Canada south to northern South America. The various species and subspecies inhabit swamps, deserts, and mountains. They live in a wide variety of habitats capable of supporting reptiles. They have the largest natural geographical range of any land snake and live from below sea level to over a mile high.

Origin of Captive Specimens

Many kingsnakes are still being collected in the wild. Some, like the Louisiana Milksnake (*L. t. amaura*) are easily collected in winter when the swamps freeze by splitting open decomposing logs above the frozen water line. Many subspecies are collected by the non-habitat destructive technique of "road cruising." You simply drive slowly at night through suitable habitat and watch for the kingsnakes on or near the road, or "spot light" nearby banks, ditches, etc. This is most effective during early summer nights. The Eastern Milksnake (*L. t. triangulum*) and the Scarlet Kingsnake (*L. t. elapsoides*) are two U.S. subspecies of milksnake which are still commonly collected in some numbers from the wild for the general pet trade. Fortunately several thousand of the larger kingsnake subspecies are now produced annually in captivity. Many of the mountain species are collected in the rocks. If not careful a lot of habitat destruction can result from their collection. Please replace rocks, logs, etc. as close to where they were when you found them. It hurts to go into an area where habitat has been ruthlessly destroyed, and many unfortunate laws have been passed which limits our ability to possess these snakes because of the damage someone has done. In meadow or grassy fields, boards can be placed about the area. After a year or so "seasoning" you can visit these boards and find all sorts of wildlife, including snakes that have made homes under them. As a general rule, I would strongly recommend the purchase of a parasite and disease-free, acclimated, captive-produced animal over the acquisition of a wild-caught animal. This has the added benefit of being able to talk to the breeder about the care needed for that specific snake and its history, feeding records, etc.

Size

As you would guess with 50 plus species and subspecies spread over such a large area, the adult sizes of the kingsnakes vary. Some of the smaller North American subspecies are adult at 18 inches while some of the Central and South American forms reach nearly six feet in length. Rare individuals of some of the kingsnakes have reached an impressive 7 feet in length.

Color Variations and Patterns

Most of the 25 recognized subspecies of milksnakes are remarkably similar, many bearing a theme of bands around the body (with variations in numbers and widths) of three basic colors: red/orange, yellow/white, and black. There is one subspecies from Central America (*L. t. gaigae*) that hatches as a tricolor then turns solid black as an adult. The Eastern Milksnake (*L. t. triangulum*) looks more blotched than banded with tricolor rings. There are also some unusual color "morphs" being produced in captivity (striped, solid colors, unusual patterns, etc.) and you can expect more unusual combinations to be produced in the future. Some *triangulum* subspecies have been cross-bred with each other. Some of the other kingsnakes may be all black, black/brown and white/yellow rings around the body, some with lengthwise stripes. With so many forms, almost any snake you find could be a kingsnake. And a few have been interbred with other species and even genera, so expect almost anything to show up on the pet market. I prefer to keep the subspecies "pure" and trace lineage to avoid breeding siblings where possible, although most combinations can make good captives. Be aware that even the scientific experts can't always identify all the wild-caught animals to the sub-specific level. If this is important to you, be selective and either capture your own or get yours from a reputable breeder. If you chose to capture your own, be sure to check with local regulations, many reptiles, including kingsnakes are protected or their take is regulated in some way.

Sex Determination

This is very important. Imagine how you would feel if you decided to buy some baby snakes, expensive ones, to raise and breed. Three years later you find some of your "girls" are boys. And even when

Beautiful Brook's Kingsnakes, *Lampropeltis getula brooksi*. Photo by Bill Love.

there is an "honest mistake" usually a boy is mistaken for a girl. Verify you get what you expect, you can't go back. There is no obvious sexual dimorphism in kingsnakes (external differences between male and female). To determine the sex of juveniles, a male's hemipenes can be everted by, starting 3/4" to 1" past the vent on the underside of the tail, applying gentle pressure with your thumb and rolling towards the vent. This method isn't foolproof, but if you see hemipenes you will know that a particular animal is a male. If nothing "pops" (the process of manually everting the hemipenes is called "popping") you should still use a very small probe to confirm the sex of a probable female because the hemipenes don't always evert with this method. Males probe to a greater depth than females, but you need someone to show you how to do this safely.

With adults, a sexing probe will be needed to determine sex accurately. Rather than describe the process of probing, again it is recommended that you find an experienced individual to show you how. A snake can be severely injured by improper application of the procedure. Experienced herpetoculturists and sales personnel at specialty reptile stores should be happy to demonstrate it for you on a prospective purchase.

A hypomelanistic Greer's Kingsnake, Lampropeltis mexicana greeri. Photo by Don Soderberg.

Growth rate and reproduction: Most snakes grow all their lives, although the majority of their growth will be in the first few years of life. With optimal conditions and unlimited food, most kingsnakes can reach adult size and reproduce in two years. Some female kingsnakes will start breeding at two years and will continue laying one to three clutches of eggs for the next eight to ten years. Others will also start laying at two years of age but ultimately will become stunted and never really do well or grow to a large size. It would be wise to wait until the third year before breeding your snake. Many baby kingsnakes will "go off" food during the winter months. This time period coincides with their natural brumation (hibernation) cycle. If this happens I put the babies in the cool room with the adults and brumate them over the winter. Usually it will take 3-4 years for these to reach safe breeding size. I feel size, not age, is the determining factor for breeding, so if your snake grows to adult size quickly, great, but if it grows slow it will take a while. I have had some kingsnake males breed at 9 months of age, many females at 2 years.

Chapter TWO: Housing and Maintenance

A nicely decorated *Lampropeltis* cage. Photo by Jill Griffith.

Cages can be as elaborate and decorative, or as simple as you want to make them. Obviously a cage suitable for a baby kingsnake will be different than that required by a pair or colony of adult breeder kingsnakes. What should be considered the basic herpetocultural requirements for any size kingsnake?

1) An escape proof enclosure designed for keeping snakes.

2) Adequate ventilation.

3) A shelter.

4) A range of temperatures (establishing temperature gradients) within the enclosure which allows for voluntary thermoregulation.

5) Water (except temporarily when treating a medical problem).

6) Food at regular intervals to allow for growth and a healthy maintenance of weight.

SELECTING AN ENCLOSURE

There are many commercially produced reptile cages suitable for your kingsnake(s). They include customized all-glass aquaria with sliding screen tops that lock, glass and wood enclosures with front or top openings, and all fiberglass cages with overlapping sliding glass front openings that lock, to describe a few. With top-opening cages you will usually be better able to control and contain a quick-moving kingsnake, but front-opening cages are acceptable. They should be well ventilated. Avoid cages with fine screen sides or low screen openings. The snake may rub its nose raw by sliding and pushing its snout against the screen. Be sure the cage is secure and "escape-proof" as kingsnakes will test every possible opening. Check your pet and reptile shops for the latest selection in caging or consult with the supplier of your snake and build your own.

Size of Enclosure

Avoid extreme sizes. If an enclosure is too large, a snake can become "lost in it" making it generally difficult to monitor its overall health and behaviors. A snake in an enclosure that is too large and poorly designed may also stay at one end, hidden, and not venture

A unique but simple setup where aquariums are slid up against heat tape under lights. Photo by Bob Applegate.

forth to seek out food items. On the other hand, too small an enclosure will result in a snake that will be cramped, lying in its own feces, and unable to utilize heat gradients. A small cage will also "foul" faster and be more difficult to keep clean and properly ventilated. The proper cage is one where if the snake were to crawl around the perimeter, it would cover approximately half the perimeter measurement, with a reasonable width to length ratio (no long skinny cages!) A good general rule is a width approximately one third of the length of the snake. Although kingsnakes will occasionally climb, tall cages are not essential for their maintenance. A standard 5 gallon vivarium will be large enough for maintaining a hatchling snake up to a year. A standard 20 gallon high or 15 gallon low vivarium (12" wide x 24" long) will be a suitable minimum size for all but the largest subspecies of adult kingsnakes. Large species\subspecies such as Honduran Milksnakes and Florida Kingsnakes will require Commercial enclosures at least 30 inches long.

Temperature

As a rule, snakes will fare better when they are provided with a choice of temperature gradients. Snakes will thermoregulate by selecting desired temperature gradients. Having temperature gradients with 75°F at one end of the enclosure and 88°F at the other is ideal. In enclosures where temperature gradients have been established, the behaviors of snakes will often yield clues to their preferred temperature ranges or to flaws in the established gradients. If they are always at the cool end, then it is possible that the warm end may be too hot. If they are always on the heated end, then there probably isn't enough heat being provided.

There are many commercial bottom or subcage heating tapes, pads, strips, and devices currently available in the general pet trade that will provide the desired temperatures. Most can be controlled with a rheostat (light dimmer)or better yet a variable thermostat that regulates electrical flow to maintain an exact temperature independent of what the room temperatures are, so you can lower the surface temperature if necessary. Avoid the "hot brick" that plops in the cage. The temperature is too localized and the surface temperature on many exceeds what is recommended and can burn your snake. At the time of writing, there are heaters with thermostatic controls which may be more suitable for keeping kingsnakes, and companies are always coming out with newer better products, so shop around for your needs. Use a thermometer to assess the surface temperature of these heaters, and your cage areas in general.

Lights are not generally recommended as a heat source because kingsnakes are not usually a basking species.

A commercially available heat mat. Photo by Edison Gabrintina.

Factors including choice of incandescent bulb, placement of the light, and vivarium design will play a key role in determining the effectiveness of using lights as a source of radiant heat. As a general rule, sub-floor heat is preferable so the snakes can lay over it and warm themselves. When your "heater device" is installed, check floor temperatures frequently and adjust until it has stabilized where you want it. If you must settle for a constant overall cage temperature, 80°F-86°F is recommended. If possible, check with your reptile dealer for the "latest and best" in cage heating devices. This is an area of critical importance in assuring the welfare of your snake and warrants special attention.

Water

Let's face it . . . Snakes in the wild don't have 24/7 access to fresh water. Often they go a long time inbetween drinks. But they can also go underground into a moist burrow to conserve moisture. In captivity, giving fresh water once or twice a week is sufficient and letting the water in the bowl dry up will kill some diseases in the water. For adults, I like to offer fresh water in a container large enough for the snake to soak in, without overflowing, once a week.

A simple shoebox setup for a young snake. Note the feeding card for this *Lampropeltis zonata*, the California Mountain Kingsnake. Photo by Bob Applegate.

Then, if it stays clean, let it dry, then refill a week later. Clean the bowl at once if the snake defecates in it.

For babies I use the Tupperware-type plastic bowls with the lids with a one-inch hole cut in the top. These reduce evaporation inside the smaller shoe boxes, keeping them dry but allowing the snake to drink and soak at will. The diameter is such that they are wider than the cage is high so they can't overturn. Be sure the volume of the snake plus the water won't fill the container to the top or sometimes the snake can't find the hole and can drown. If the cage is taller than the width of the bowl, particularly on paper or a smooth substrate, the container can flip over and trap and suffocate the snake inside. Used properly, these water containers are great!

Lighting

No additional light is needed if the cage is in a room with windows and indirect natural light. **CAUTION:** Do not put your cage in or

A natural substrate and shelter can provide an exciting and interesting enclosure for a pet snake. This is a young *Lampropeltis pyromelana*. Photo by Jill Griffith.

near a window where the sun will shine directly on it. The interior cage temperature can rapidly rise to fatal levels, even with a ventilated top. For display purposes, there is no harm in enhancing the snakes' colors or the appeal of the vivarium design by using full spectrum bulbs such as Vita-Lite®. Remember however, that lights do produce varying amounts of heat, so be certain your light application doesn't upset your temperature balance.

Note: Kingsnakes should be provided with a period of darkness. This will be difficult if you decide to use lights as the primary heat source.

Substrate

Many kingsnakes like to burrow. You should provide a layer of sand, small smooth gravel, wood chips, pine shavings, or aspen bedding (not cedar or other "oily" woods) as a ground medium or substrate for the bottom of your enclosure. Some kingsnakes (Scarlet Kingsnakes and others) do better when their cage is half full of dry sphagnum moss. They will hide in and burrow through the moss.

Many safe substrate materials for kingsnakes are available at pet stores. Photo by Ryan Moss.

When a cup containing baby mice (pinkies) is placed on the surface of the moss, the snakes emerge (often at night) and eat the pinkies. Sometimes this is the only way to get these snakes to readily accept pinkies as food. **CAUTION:** Some milk snakes have developed a sticky, blister-type premature shed skin problem when kept in damp moss. If this problem occurs, change to a different substrate.

Shelters

Kingsnakes like to hide and fare better when provided with a secure place where they can be out of sight. Actually, two shelters per cage is recommended, one at the warm end and one at the cool end. Then the snake can be at its temperature of choice and not compromise its desire to be hidden. For example, a snake digesting a meal may prefer to be warm and hidden. If the only shelter was at the cool end of the cage, the snake may choose to hide and could develop digestion problems associated with cool temperatures.

There are many attractive, natural-looking, and easy to clean shelters available from your pet store. You can also use something as simple as a cereal box or small plastic container with a hole cut into it. The diameter of the entrance should be a bit larger than the diameter of

A simple setup using a ten-gallon terrarium and a securely fitting screen top. Add a heat pad and you'll have all you need. Photo by Bob Applegate.

the largest snake. Snakes like to squeeze into tight places. Don't use an excessively large shelter. One that is "snug" with an apparent inside volume 1-1/2 - 2 times the apparent volume of the snake is great. If there is more than one snake inside the cage, use a shelter that will be large enough for both of them to fit inside, plus one more. Be sure a well-fed snake can comfortably coil inside.

Large Scale HOUSING

BABY KINGSNAKES

Over the years I have tried many cage systems in which to raise baby snakes. A primary consideration should be to keep baby snakes singly in their own cages. Feeding "accidents" occur when one baby eats another cage mate. If you are going to work with large numbers of baby snakes, simple, easy-to-monitor and easy-to-maintain caging will be a must.

A rack of plastic shoe boxes has proven an efficient and widely used system for maintaining large numbers of baby snakes (see illustration). I use custom-built racks which each hold 160 plastic

Room full of baby racks. Note the proportional thermostats, each controlling two rows. Photo by Bob Applegate.

shoe boxes (clear plastic storage containers measuring 3.5" x 7" x 12"). I recommend the clear plastic boxes with clear lids. It is much nicer when you can see down through the top before you open it. Each rack is built so that, when a shoe box is put on a shelf, the shelf above holds the lid in place. Several 1/8" holds are drilled in the sides and ends of each shoe box for ventilation. For heat, grooves are cut lengthwise in the upper surface of each shelf that will be under a row of shoe boxes, about 4" from the rear of the 11" wide shelves, and about 1" wide. Heat tape is installed flush with the top in these channels. Holes are drilled in the rack's end pieces to allow the heat tape to drop down and heat a second shelf. Each heat tape covers two shelves (20 shoe boxes) and is wired to variable thermostat, then through a master room temperature thermostat (set at 82°F). The shelves are then covered with sheet metal for heat dispersal and fire safety.(My newer shelves now have aluminum channel over the heat tape, same idea cleaner look.) This setup gives you quite a bit of control, and gives the snakes quite a bit of choice. You can increase or decrease the temperature of the warm area above the heat tape. The snakes can move forward into the 1" area of the shoe box in front of the shelf for cooler temperatures, to the rear for warmth. If all the snakes are always in front, the cage is too hot and the heat should be turned down. In my system, boxes can be individually

A drawer system unit for housing a large number of adult kingsnakes. Photo by Bob Applegate.

controlled in lots of 20, so some can be warmer or cooler, depending on the snakes' requirements. With the master thermostat, if the room heats up, the tapes will turn off, but not until the room reaches a nice safe 82°F.

Inside each shoe box is a substrate of hardwood chips, walnut (crushed) or pine shavings. I have used all with success. A folded paper serves as a hiding place, and a small plastic container with a 1" hole cut in the top serves as the water dish. The water container is wider than the inside height of the shoe box, so it can't be overturned. The small hole in the top reduces the amount of evaporation and promotes a drier interior in the shoe box.

SUBADULT KINGSNAKES

In addition to the shoe boxes, I also have a rack of 48 medium-sized storage boxes. These are larger versions of the shoe boxes (about twice the floor space) and can be used as an intermediate step after the shoe boxes, but before the cages for adult-sized snakes. They can also be used as quarantine enclosures. All new snakes should go through a quarantine of at least 30 days, until you are certain that they are healthy and it is safe to add them to an existing collection. This rack is set up like the shoe box rack, with thermostatically

Detail of the cage unit showing drawers in which the snakes feel secure. Photo by Bob Applegate.

controlled heat tape. The shelves are wider and spaced further apart to accommodate the larger boxes.

ADULT KINGSNAKES

There are several alternatives to the large-scale housing of breeding-age kingsnakes. Many breeders use a variation of the previously mentioned shoe box and sweater box racks, using the larger plastic storage containers which have become available in recent years. With the larger storage units, some breeders opt to remove the lids and construct shelving that allows the top edge of a plastic storage box to rest flush against an upper shelf. Essentially, the storage boxes are used as drawers in a custom-built shelf unit where the upper shelves serve as lids.

What I use for housing adult kingsnakes are the double-compartmented, drawer-type cages. They are glass-fronted, of wood construction with a double floor, including the inside of the drawer. The individual cage units measure 24" deep by 18" wide. The drawers are slightly narrower, about 3.5" in height and only 20" deep. The 4" space behind the drawer and under the rear floor of the upper-cage area provides an airspace through which a heat tape is passed. This allows for thermoregulation in the drawer and cage as described for the shoe boxes. Each row of cages has its own heat tape, and they are controlled essentially as described for the shoe boxes. The lights are fluorescent 4' that fit in the normal fixtures. Sometimes I will substitute special lights just to experiment or enhance colors (the ballasts are removed and reinstalled remotely to avoid hot spots) set above the 1/8" mesh covered openings on the top of the cages. The lights are on timers and also connected to a room temperature thermostat.

The "hole" to the drawer is a raised 1.5" PVC pipe. It extends 1" above the floor to prevent the substrate from the upper level from dropping into the drawer. Coarse silica sand, #3 gravel, and various wood chip products can be used as a substrate with no problems. I have used many substrates over the years, I really liked the silica sand (even though I had to wash it constantly to eliminate dust) because I could see the "sperm plugs" after mating which helped in the breeding efforts (to be covered later). I have now switched to T-Rex Calci-Sand®. The maintenance is much easier than with most other substrates and safer for me and the snakes (no silica dust). Once a year, I remove the Calci-Sand®, sift out particles (feces), soak it in bleach for 24 hours (this also "sets" the FDA food colors used in the non-white colors), rinse thoroughly, sun dry (the cage is sterilized at this time), and replace the cage. The rest of the year I just spot clean and I can still see the sperm plugs.

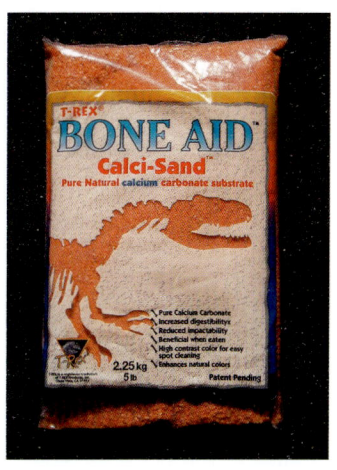

Avoid any chemically treated substrate like "kitty litter" and avoid the oily woods like cedar and redwood. A hide box and water crock are provided in the upper compartment. Normally there are two snakes kept per cage. During feeding a cap is placed over the PVC pipe and the snakes are segregated such that one snake is left in the drawer and the other in the upper compartment until each has completed feeding.

Room full of split level drawer system cages. Photo by Bob Applegate.

In addition to the above-mentioned setup, I have a second room with similar but smaller drawer-type cages. The room temperature is thermostatically controlled and heated by incandescent lights. The cages in this room, however, do not include any type of lighting. Whatever light is available originates from some natural light through the windows and fluorescent bulbs on the ceiling which are left on and off at random, sometimes for days at a time. I have had equally good results with breeding kingsnakes in this setup as I have with the fancy ones with all the timers and special lights. Because of the successful breeding results over many years and other factors known to me, I don't believe that light cycles or special lights are needed to successfully raise, keep, and breed kingsnakes. Full-spectrum lights will enhance the display appeal of kingsnakes and their enclosures, but they are not required for their successful husbandry and propagation.

My newest experiment in caging is something to behold! Split level condominiums for snakes. On the upper level there are two glass doors on two cages measuring 2feet by 2 feet by 16 inches high. There are three "kitty litter" type plastic drawers under the two cages. If the caps are off the raised pvc access"holes" in the floor, the snakes can go from the drawer on the right up into the cage, down into the middle drawer under the divider, then up into the left cage then down into the left drawer. But this is not all! The lower level is the same, except there are pvc pipes in the ceiling that allow the snakes to climb from the lower cages to the upper, so all in all a snake can access 4 glass fronted cages and 6 drawers.

Heat tape is set up as previously described. I can now keep colonies of up to 10 kingsnakes in one "system". I don't need as many males, can isolate in any combination for feeding, egg laying, etc, and it gives the snakes more exercise. This new room has been in operation a few years now and I am very happy with the results. And, no, cannabalism has not been a problem, except for feeding and egg laying the colonies live together 24/7. Do not try a colony of baby kingsnakes, however, and during the establishment of the colony, watch the introductions for a while to make sure they are compatable. Some kingsnakes will accept more than one male in a colony, others will not. Some species or individuals will not do well in a colony situation and will have to be kept as individuals.

What has been presented so far in caging will allow you to accommodate large numbers of all ages and sizes of kingsnakes and produce hundreds of babies each year. It is by necessity an "assembly line" type operation where one can move rapidly from cage to cage and service the occupants. There are many good cages sold in shops that are perfectly adequate for housing a limited number of kingsnakes. You could convert a TV cabinet into a living room showcase for snakes, or a small cage or aquarium with a locking lid will also work well. Just remember to supply the snake's basic needs: clean, dry cage, fresh water, a hiding place, good ventilation, and temperature gradient from approximately 75°F to about 88°F.

An incredible naturalistic setup. Photo by Kevin McCurley.

ON NATURALISTIC DISPLAYS

Although I have so far described simple, efficient systems for maintaining kingsnakes, this should not imply that you can't build a large cage and design an elaborate "natural" interior with plants, rock piles, etc. Remember, however, that kingsnakes are shy and will remain hidden most of the time. They also like to burrow and will constantly "redesign" your interior. A word of caution. Any heavy objects used in a vivarium, such as rock piles and water bowls, should rest directly on the cage floor. If kingsnakes are allowed to burrow under heavy objects they may push the substrate from beneath and allow the heavy object to crush them to death.

Chapter THREE: Your Pet Kingsnake

Developing A Pet / Owner Relationship

Kingsnakes are beautiful, relatively small, and make wonderful captive animals. However, many are nervous, jumpy, and often prefer to remain hidden. There are always exceptions, but many milk snakes will not make good pets if your primary goal is to handle and "play" with your snake. The juveniles are especially nervous, sometimes calming down only when they reach a larger adult size.

For a variety of reasons, kingsnakes and milksnakes are some of the best pet snakes available in the hobby. John Mack photographed by Bob Ashley.

Gentle, regular handling is the best bet if you want to try to habituate your snake to handling. Some milk snakes will not calm down no matter what you try. Many of the other kingsnakes will make better pets. Some of the rock dwelling species, such as the Arizona Mountain Kingsnakes and Gray-banded Kingsnakes seem to handle better. Perhaps their climbing habits make them "cling" to their owner better than some of the "run to escape predators" open area dwellers.

Because each is an individual, with different behavioral traits, you should consider the following: There are two lives to consider with

The bite of a small kingsnake, in this case an albino Common Kingsnake, *Lampropeltis getula*, is medically of no consequence. Treat it as a scratch. Photo by Jill Griffith.

regards to handling. The first is yours. If a kingsnake doesn't bite you, or defecate all over you or your furniture, handling the snake will not cause you any harm. If, after being handled, a snake doesn't regurgitate meals, continues to feed, and behaves in a relatively calm manner then occasional handling will probably not be harmful to your snake. However, it is advisable not to handle your snake after a meal (as long as you can see the lump) or when it is opaque or just before shedding. The reason being if a snake desides to "run" to escape, it will want to be as fast as possible. A food lump will slow it down, so it may decide to regurgitate to speed up its escape. When a snake is opaque the skin is easily damaged and often it is more nervous because its vision is impaired.

Before Buying A Kingsnake

Before buying a kingsnake you should consider your reasons for wanting to own a snake. If your primary reason is owning a snake that you can regularly handle, select a larger species/subspecies which tend to be a little more calm. Many milk snake subspecies

Even this small Honduran Milksnake can become quite tame with some handling. Photo by Bill Love.

may not be the best possible choice (see previous section on handling). Snakes also have certain environmental and feeding requirements which need to be addressed prior to purchase. There are many people who like snakes but cannot cope with the issue of feeding rodents. Other reptiles would probably be a better choice for these individuals. However, if you are looking for a beautiful, moderate-sized, relatively easily maintained and docile species of snake, few can be more highly recommended than the kingsnakes with their shiny scales, clearly defined patterns and vivid colors.

SELECTING A POTENTIALLY HEALTHY Kingsnake

It is not possible to be 100% sure of the health status of a snake or its adaptability to captive conditions. However, by following certain steps in the initial selection of a snake, the probability for success will be considerably increased.

The following are recommended guidelines for selection:

1) Inspect the snake and pay attention to its apparent weight. A healthy snake has a rounded tapering cylindrical body, with no outlines of the ribs or backbone clearly apparent.

2) Look at the skin. It should be "full," clean, shiny, and with no wounds, bumps, blisters, or damp sticky areas.

3) Ask to handle the snake. A healthy snake is active and gives a sense of muscular vigor when moving through a hand. A limp-feeling snake is usually an unhealthy snake. Many vendors at reptile shows will not let anyone handle their snakes at the show. Often at shows there are imports and potentially diseased snakes. If you have handled other reptiles prior to arriving at a vendors table, and handle his/her snake, you could cause a disease or parasite transfer, so respect the no. If you are a serious cash ready customer, usually the vendor will have you clean your hands with some sort of sterilizing agent, then handle the snake, but understand the reluctance. Often vendors have many years work in the developement of his/her "products" and the only exposure to disease is at these shows.

4) Let the snake crawl through your fingers. Apply firm but gentle resistance to the snake's movement and feel for broken ribs or any irregular lumps or cavities in the body.

5) Examine the head area. The eye caps should be clear and the pupils in both eyes should be the same.

6) Inspect around the eyes and between the chin scales for mites, and all over the body for ticks.

7) Gently open the mouth (using a blunt instrument) and look for discoloration, "cheesy" matter (sign of mouth rot), or any signs of infection or injury. Look for excessive phlegm or bubbly mucus in the mouth. If present, this symptom combined with others such as gaping or forced exhalations suggests the presence of respiratory disorders or infections.

8) Examine the underside of the snake. Look for scars or discoloration of scales. Closely examine the vent area for any signs of diarrhea, swelling, or crusty accumulations. The anal plate of a healthy snake will lie flat against the body.

9) After replacing the snake in its cage, immediately inspect your hands for any crawling mites.

A beautiful dark morph *Lampropeltis alterna*, Gray-banded Kingsnake. Photo by Bob Applegate.

10) Ask to see any food records and/or talk to the vendor about the history of that specific snake.

If the snake is a prospective purchase and there are any problems found, don't even consider buying the animal. It is a good idea, before concluding a purchase, to ask the seller about the snake's habits, food preferences, date of last shed, and anything unusual about the snake. If possible ask to watch the snake feed. Remember that, as a general rule, a captive-hatched and/or raised snake maintained in a clean, sanitary environment will have a much better chance of establishing in captivity than a wild-caught snake. If the snake is captive-hatched, ask if it is possible to see the parents. To a significant degree, the characteristics of the parents will provide you with a good idea of what you can expect your snake to become. If a decision is made to buy the snake, consider having a veterinarian check for internal parasites, particularly if it was wild-caught. Consider who you buy it from, will they be there for questions/help, later on?

FIRST CLUTCH VERSUS SECOND OR THIRD CLUTCH BABIES

Is there an advantage to buying first clutch animals over second or third clutch hatchlings? The answer is yes, but not for what is often suspected to be the reason. Second or third clutch animals can be just as healthy, large, and vigorous as first clutch animals. The time and season of purchase, however, can play a key role in determining how soon a captive-raised snake will be able to breed. The primary reason that first-clutch animals are preferable when available is that you will have more time to grow them, and thus, will be more likely to have them close to adult size by their second winter when they will be cooled for the first time prior to attempted breeding. Second or third clutch snakes born late in the season will have fewer months of feeding and growth available prior to that initial cooling, two winters down the line. However, purchasing later clutch animals this year is preferable to purchasing first clutch animals next year for the same reasons. Because yearling snakes often will not feed their second winter and need to be hibernated, even if still small, it may take 2.5-3 years to grow and breed second or third clutch animals, but they should be larger and capable of producing more eggs with fewer risks than the next year's first clutch animals.

ACCLIMATION OF YOUR NEW SNAKE

Once you bring your new snake home, you should set up a properly designed enclosure to accommodate your new snake. If you own other snakes, your new snake should be housed in a separate and isolated room for at least 30 days and preferably 60-90 days. Thus the acclimation period will also serve as a quarantine period.

Initially, leave the snake alone in the cage for two or three days then offer a small meal that won't leave a lump in the snake. Do not handle or disturb the snake for a couple of days after the meal. Three or four days later, offer a second meal. Do not handle the snake until the snake has fed at least three times. The acclimation period will allow you to make some assessments about the health of the snake. A snake that regurgitates its meals may have a gastroenteric disease. If you handle a snake, you have to consider the fact that the stress of handling may be causing it to regurgitate.

This can make it difficult for you to assess the cause of regurgitation. Another thing you will be looking for during the acclimation period is the condition of the feces. If the feces are watery, runny, or stained with blood, your snake may have a gastroenteric disease which will have to be diagnosed through a veterinary examination. As a general rule, it is recommended that a fecal check for internal parasites be performed during the acclimation period.

Finally during this time, you will be able to clearly assess whether the snake harbors mites. As any snake keeper knows, mites once introduced into a collection can be persistent and difficult to completely eradicate but, if contained in an isolated quarantine area, are easily controlled and eradicated. If buying captive hatched babies from a reputable breeder some of these steps won't be necessary, but it is a good idea for you to be aware of them anyway.

In summary, the acclimation/quarantine period will allow you to assess the following:

1. Overall health and behavior.

2. That a snake is feeding.

3. That a snake is not regurgitating.

4. The apparent status of the feces and probability of gastroenteric disease.

5. The presence of mites.

Chapter Four: Feeding

A black and white California Kingsnake feeding on a small mouse. Photo by Jill Griffith.

In the wild there are records of kingsnakes eating a variety of vertebrates and invertebrates. The preferred foods will vary with the species/subspecies, possibly within populations of a subspecies, and depending on food choices available, probably from individual to individual. From a strictly practical standpoint, we will focus on feeding kingsnakes prey animals readily available to us as snake keepers: primarily commercially raised rodents.

The adults of the larger species/subspecies of kingsnakes can and will eat baby rabbits and/or birds, but most kingsnakes will thrive in captivity on a diet of mice and rats. There are some subspecies that are too small to eat a newborn mouse (pinkie) when first hatched. These species/subspecies are best avoided, or accepted as a challenge, to see if you can find solutions for satisfying their particular dietary needs, at least until they become large enough to eat "pinkies." A good example of this type of kingsnake is the beautiful Scarlet Kingsnake (*L. t. elapsoides*). One of the reasons that this in-demand subspecies of milksnake is not widely bred in captivity is that the tiny babies are notoriously difficult to feed.

FEEDING SCHEDULE FOR HATCHLINGS AND SUBADULTS

We will start the methodology of feeding with a baby kingsnake just after its first shed. Soon after hatching, a baby kingsnake can be offered a newborn mouse. It is, however, rare that the food will be accepted and eaten. Normally, a hatchling snake won't accept food until after its first shed, usually 6-14 days after hatching. After the first shed the snake should accept its first meal within two to three weeks. The first meal should be small enough to be easily swallowed, but large enough to leave a visible lump in the snake after being swallowed. A schedule of one feeding per week, with the size of food gradually increasing as the snake grows, will result in a good growth rate.

A young Arizona Mountain Kingsnake eating a pink mouse. Photo by Jill Griffith.

However, many herpetoculturists are in a hurry to grow hatchlings into adult breeders, so they will often adopt a feeding schedule consisting of offering an undersized mouse three times a week instead of a larger mouse once a week. Three smaller meals seem to produce better growth (more easily digested and allows for ingesting a greater total weight of food in a given time span than a single large meal), and be accepted more readily than one large one. It is normal for a snake to skip a meal or two every so often when offered food this frequently. If a kingsnake continues to accept meals, it can be fed through its first winter (make sure to keep the snake warm) and

A California Kingsnake eating a mouse. Photo by Bob Applegate.

through the following spring, summer, and fall. It can then be cooled during the second winter of its life if you feel it has reached breedable size, or it stops feeding on its own at this time. The following spring you should be able, following a return to normal maintenance and feeding schedule, to attempt to breed it.

As long as they are growing larger and longer you can't overfeed a baby snake. If one should regurgitate, give it a few days rest, then feed it small meals once a week until it gets back on track. With this intensive feeding schedule, babies will usually outgrow the shoe box in the first year.

Don't be surprised if baby kingsnakes refuse a meal when opaque. This is normal in many cases but offer a smaller-than-usual meal anyway. Many kingsnakes will eat when opaque, but you don't want to offer a food item that creates a large lump in the snake because it might hinder the shedding process. Sometimes when you move a snake to a larger or different cage its feeding pattern will be disrupted. Some snakes are more secure and eat better when in a confined space and don't readily feed when placed in larger quarters. If this happens, you may have to put them in a confined space or back into their previous cage setup to feed until they get used to their new environment.

Note: In some countries it is illegal to feed live or non natural live (not from the natural range of the snake) food to captive snakes. Considering we poison and trap mice all the time, I don't see how feeding a live baby mouse to your snake should violate anything, but check for local laws, and your choice, either follow them or don't tell anybody!

FEEDING ADULTS

Once the snake reaches adult size you will want to offer enough food to keep up continued growth and body weight, but not so much as to cause obesity. The relationship of food intake to length and weight increases will vary from individual to individual. Some kingsnakes will "eat like pigs" and stay slim, while others will not consume as much, but get fat. If the scales are always stretched apart, or if the inside edge of a coil wrinkles or folds when a snake curls up, the snake is probably too fat.

Always keep snakes separate when feeding. If you are using the double-compartmented, drawer-type cages, feed one in the upper compartment and the other in the lower compartment, and cap the access hole. **DO NOT FEED GROUPS OF SNAKES TOGETHER IN THE SAME ENCLOSURE.**

With males, one meal per week is usually enough during the "warm" season. During the breeding season males may skip several meals (one- track minds, sex only?). Monitor males during this period for noticeable weight loss and review their feeding records. If continued disinterest in feeding is likely to jeopardize a male snake's health, he may have to be moved to a cage by himself, perhaps to a separate room away from the "aroma" of the females before he will resume feeding. If your records indicate a repetitive pattern of extended fasting during the breeding season, you will want to adjust your feeding regimen and offer a male snake additional meals during its feeding phase to provide extra weight gain in preparation for this fast.

Female kingsnakes that are expected to lay eggs can be a little on the plump side. Unless obviously overweight, try to offer meals to adult females twice per week. When opaque prior to laying eggs, offer smaller delicacies. If a normal meal is a full-grown mouse, offer a pinkie rat or young fuzzy mouse. Some females will accept food between the pre-egg laying shed and the actual egg laying, even eating a small food animal the day the eggs are laid. It is also common for sexually mature, gravid females to go off feed completely. Offer food frequently because if they didn't eat today they may eat tomorrow. Having something continually digesting is the "secret formula" to getting kingsnakes to lay two and sometimes three clutches of eggs per year. Egg production causes significant depletion of a female's bodily reserves and anything you can do to help her replenish them will be beneficial to her.

Stop feeding of adults two weeks before planning to drop the temperatures for "hibernation." (Yes I know the correct term is brumation, but old habits are hard to break, and brumating sounds like something a cow should be doing in a field). This will allow most of the stomach contents to be digested and eliminated before the cooling period. Because the metabolic rate of snakes slows down when they are cooled, any undigested food can decompose and cause a harmful buildup of bacteria in the gastrointestinal tract.

FEEDING PROBLEMS

Now and then, there is a snake that refuses to eat what we offer it. Most adult kingsnakes should already have a feeding history by the time you get them, so what follows will focus on the newly hatched baby snake. By using larger portions the following guidelines can also be applied to adult or subadult snakes.

Before proceeding with methods for dealing with problem feeders, be aware that some baby snakes, for a variety of reasons, are destined to die. They may be deformed internally, unable to digest food, or have some other defects that will prevent a prolonged life. Fortunately, these are rare occurrences.

Before we can expect a problem snake to feed, and before we can tackle the problem, a short review of husbandry is in order. We must provide a suitable environment, preferably a small cage so the snake can't avoid the food item. The cage should be clean, dry, a 75°-88°F temperature (preferably with subfloor heat with warmer and cooler areas available), have clean drinking water, a suitable substrate, and a secure place to hide in both the warm and cool zones. The snake should be kept alone and all food items should be of a size that can be easily swallowed without leaving a large lump in the snake. The

A "banana" or high yellow California Kingsnake being offered a thawed mouse. Photo by Bill Love.

food item should be left in the cage for several hours and the cage should not be disturbed during that time, preferably with no one in the room. Some snakes are nocturnal feeders, so you may have to try these techniques day and night. Best results are often obtained after a shed, so delay feeding if the snake is "blue" or opaque.

The following is a summary of techniques for dealing with problem feeders:

1. Make sure that all recommended enclosure requirements are provided. Inadequate environmental factors can play a key role in the failure of snakes to feed in captivity.

2. Most babies will feed on live newborn mice (pinkies). Place a live pinkie in the opening to the snakes favorite hiding place. If uneaten within a few hours, drop the pinkie inside the hiding place with the snake. If uneaten, replace with a fresh, killed pinkie.

3. Wash a pinkie in soap (non perfumed) and water, rinse well, dry, and follow steps in number one. The washing removes the domestic mouse scent and may make it more palatable.

4. Get a freshly killed feeder lizard (*Uta, Sceloporus* or *Anolis*) and rub it all over a pre-killed pinkie, prepared as in Steps 1 and 3. You may have to cut a small piece of the lizard's tail off, rub the lizard's blood around the face of the pinkie, and put a piece of the tail in the pre-killed pinkie's mouth. Frog or worm slime may work here also and is worth a try. Some of the artificial lizard scent will also work.

5. Kill a pinkie, cut open the top of the head, smear brain material around the head, then place the pinkie in the hiding place. This grisly technique works surprisingly often, but I don't like to use it if the other techniques work.

At this point, if the snake still has not fed, offer it any natural food item you think it might accept, just to get a meal into it. Offer the item (small lizard, tree frog, baby wild mouse) by hand first. If the snake will accept food from your hand, it will be easier to offer two food items at the same time and cause the snake to "miss" its target and to take the pinkie you are holding tightly next to the preferred item. Always leave a pinkie in the cage after a snake has accepted a different food item. Often, the snake will follow the first meal with the pinkie.

Remove the snake from the cage, place it in a small paper bag or plastic cup, and try steps 1-5 again if there has been no success at this point.

Usually a snake will have fed before we reach this point, and once it has eaten, it will usually be easy to get it to accept plain pinkies. If it has not eaten yet, heavily mist the cage with a wet sprayer to raise the humidity and try the steps again. Don't keep the snake in a wet cage more than a couple of days, and be sure the cage is warm. Another method involves withholding water from the snake for a few days, then put a wet pre-killed pinkie in a shallow dish in the cage. Sometimes a plastic container filled with damp shavings and having a small entrance hole will serve as a secure hiding place and encourage a feeding response when a pinkie is dropped inside with the snake. Sometimes putting the snake in a paper bag or ventilated small cup over night with the pinkie will do the trick. Sometimes a deep substrate with an over turned container with the pinkie inside so the snake can burrow and come up under the cup to get the pinkie will help. On some of the kings, dried and powdered corn snake shed applied on a damp washed pinkie will get them feeding. Be inventive here, try anything you can think of.

Note: Some baby snakes react badly to constant contact with damp peat moss, suffering a dermatitis from the acid ground medium. Whatever material you use, keep alert for signs of skin disease when using wet media. The problem may show up as an inability to shed, a premature shed, sticking skin, or as skin blisters. These lesions, when healed, may leave discolored scales or scars. Damp paper towel is a good choice as a temporary, moist substrate.

FORCE FEEDING

If your snake has not eaten 4 weeks after its first shed, you may have to force feed it. Kill a day-old pinkie and gently stick the head inside the snake's mouth, using the pinkie's head (or other small dull object) to open the snake's mouth. When the pinkie's head is inside the snake's mouth, gently apply pressure to the outside of the upper and lower jaws of the snake with your fingers and gently pull on the pinkie. This will stick the pinkie on the snake's teeth and make it more difficult for the snake to spit the pinkie out. Wait until the snake is not struggling, gently put it down in the cage, and don't move! You may have to repeat this several times but often the snake will accept and swallow the pinkie. If this first approach at force feeding fails after a couple of tries, start the pinkie down the same way, then gently shove the pinkie down the snake's throat using a dull instrument. Gently massage the pinkie down the snake's throat to a distance of one quarter to one third the snake's length. If a pinkie is too large for a snake, try a section of mouse tail (the mouse must be humanely killed first). Force feeding sections of mouse tails is a relatively low stress method which works well with baby eastern milk snakes and other small subspecies. When feeding a section (use a section about the length or slightly longer than the body length of a pinkie) of mouse tail, make sure that you insert the thick end of the tail first so that the bristly hairs lie flat against the tail (don't go against the lie of the hair) as it is introduced.

PINKIE PUMPS

If you have several problem feeders and don't have suitably sized food items, or, if you have a pinkie shortage and need to feed many with a few, or don't have time to "play" with feeding problems, you may want to consider using "pinkie pumps". These allow one to force feed small snakes pre-killed pinkies. "Pinkie pumps" are expensive but will pay for themselves if they allow you to save just one valuable snake. They can be used to force feed baby snakes assembly-line style and keep them alive and growing until they will accept pinkies on their own or grow large enough to accept larger food items. "Pinkie pumps" are available from specialty reptile stores or from mail order companies.

Most kingsnakes that hatch will readily feed on pinkies from the start, so the other "tricks" won't be necessary, but you should have an idea of that to try if a snake won't feed. Some baby snakes, particularly those hatched late in the season, will not accept pinkies until the following spring. Feed "late hatchers" a few lizards or pinkie pump them a few times, then "hibernate" them until the following spring. Usually it is not worth the effort to work with one of these problem late hatchlings over the winter. Snakes lose very little weight when hibernating, and if a snake has any body fat reserves, it will be fine until the following spring. Usually, with spring comes an appetite and a much better chance for easy success.

Shedding

Many animals, including humans, shed their skin. Snakes will normally shed their skin in one piece. If they have difficulty in removing all or part of this skin serious problems and even death may result. Normally, when a snake starts the shed (slough, dysecdysis) process, its pattern and colors become dull with a grayish-blue overcast. When this happens the eyes cloud over to the point where you may not even be able to see the dark pupils. This condition is called by herpetoculturists "being opaque." It is caused by a secretion coming between the outer and under layers of skin loosening the outer layer of skin. When the skin layers are prepared for the shed, the opaque condition subsides and the skin pattern and colors look normal again. Within a few days after this clearing of colors, the snake should shed, hopefully in one piece. If the snake does not shed soon after the clearing of the colors, the secretion between the two layers of skin will dry and virtually glue the old skin onto the snake's body. If the entire body is covered for an extended period of time, the snake will probably die. If parts of shed skin

An adult Sinaloan Milksnake in the process of shedding. Photo by Bob Ashley.

remain, the snake may be able to survive until the next shed, which will probably occur sooner than normal. If just a portion on the end of the tail remains, it will probably constrict that section of the tail as the skin dries, cutting off circulation, and causing that part of the tail to dry up, die, and eventually break or drop off. Snakes do not regenerate their tails, so the animal will be mutilated for life.

As a rule, skin problems including wounds, diseases, etc., will increase the frequency of shedding. Presumably this is part of the healing process.

PREVENTING SHEDDING PROBLEMS

Why does a snake have problems shedding? There are theories suggesting a number of factors including poor health, dehydration, low relative humidity, keeping the environment too dry, etc. It could be one or all of these plus some other unknowns in any given situation. How can this problem be prevented? An easy method is to record when your snake is in the opaque condition. When the clearing of the opaque condition occurs, you should expect a shed within the week.

An Eastern Milksnake sheds its skin. Photo by Bill Love.

PROCEDURES FOR DEALING WITH PROBLEM SHEDS

If a partial shed occurs, we should assist the snake out of any remaining pieces. Look for the piece of shed from the head and verify that the eye "caps" have been shed. If they haven't, look for a loose piece of skin attached to the eye cap and lift up gently and pull away from the eye orbit. If no skin is available, use a finger and gently push across the eye, forcing the cap to slide into the eye orbit on one side, but exposing the edge of the cap on the other side. Hook the exposed edge with tweezers or your finger nail. Lift up and off. The cap should lift out with very little pressure. If too much time has passed and the eye caps are "glued" in place, leave them. It is better not to risk permanent injury to the snake's eyes. The snake should be alright, even though partially blind, until the next shed. If you are sure the eye cap will come off, but can't get hold of it, sometimes touching it with tape and pulling away will remove it.

For the rest of the body with skin left, pretend that the skin is a woman's stocking. Find the edge nearest the head and roll it back towards the tail. If it seems to be stuck, it keeps tearing, or you suspect that an entire skin is still on the snake when it should have been shed off, find a round-bottomed container which the snake, when coiled in it, goes around twice. Put ventilation holes in the top, add water to a depth of one half the thickness of the snake, and place the container where it will be 82°-88°F. It may take only one hour or it may take 24 hours, but the soaking and the friction caused when the snake crawls on its own body should remove the skin. Do NOT put the snake in a cloth bag then soak it in a shallow container. The material can soak up the water to a point where it excludes air passage and the snake can smother. It is imperative that shed problems are cared for immediately on baby kingsnakes. Within a matter of 24 to 48 hours, they can go from healthy looking to dehydrated, to being on the verge of death. If the snake looks dehydrated (in fact this appearance is caused by the crinkling and adhesion of the old skin onto the new one), don't wait a week until after the opaque condition clears, start the soaking immediately.

Perhaps in the wild when kingsnakes are opaque they retreat to some moist underground hide-away which prevents any shedding problems. In the wild, a snake can also bask in the sun so the ultraviolet light can kill any bacteria on the skin. In captivity, if we keep kingsnakes too damp for extended periods of time, they end up getting skin disorders. However, a temporarily damp cage or a hide box containing a wet substrate, if made available during the shedding process, may significantly reduce the potential for shedding problems.

By closely monitoring your snakes and keeping records of when they turn opaque, you should be prepared to soak them when necessary and prevent any shedding problems.

Tongue Sheaths

Once in a while you will see what looks like a small filament of mucous membrane on a glass window of a cage. I can't prove it, but I believe these to be tongue sheds. Some research is needed here but I believe a snake sheds the skin on its tongue, but the shed is rarely found.

MONITORING SHEDDING IN BABY SNAKES

It is important that you carefully monitor shedding in baby kingsnakes. For keepers and breeders interesting in keeping detailed records, a record card can be placed on the top of each shoe box.

When you see an opaque snake, record it so you can monitor its shedding progress. If it doesn't shed soon after the eyes clear, this will alert you to a problem. Baby kingsnakes often have trouble shedding their skins when kept too dry, on the other hand, keeping them too wet can cause skin diseases. If a baby snake has problems shedding, you may have to soak it to help it shed. Baby snakes dehydrate quickly, and this "monitoring system" will save you many snakes you could easily lose to shed problems if you were to wait until they looked dried and wrinkled. I usually put snakes having problems shedding into the cage water dish with a small amount of water (a level approximately half of the thickness of a snake). Replace the lid with one that has only small ventilation holes and leave the snake to soak for a few hours to overnight. Do not place the water container directly over the heat tape area. If the skin hasn't come off during the soaking period, it should at least be soft enough that you should be able to easily remove it by hand.

As a general rule, if a snake's eyes have cleared up and a week later it hasn't shed, you should strongly consider soaking it.

FREQUENCY OF SHEDDING

Snakes shed several times per year. A baby kingsnake on a rapid growth feeding regimen may shed 12 or more times per year. Five to six times per year is normal for older kingsnakes that are being cooled over the winters for breeding. When snakes are being cooled (hibernated) they still get opaque and they still clear up and shed, but the whole process goes much slower. It may take over one month from being opaque to shedding. If the snake looks dehydrated, then you can soak it as previously described, but maintain it at the cool temperature at which the snake is being kept. Do not warm it up to soak and then return it to the cool condition.

THE EFFECT OF PHYSICAL TRAUMA DURING THE SHEDDING PROCESS

If a snake's skin is torn while opaque, or before it is ready to shed, it can be a serious problem. The skin underneath will be sticky and obviously not ready to be exposed. A small area will usually dry, scab over, then after two sheds become scarred. If the skin is accidentally torn, an antibacterial ointment can be applied to the wound. To avoid an accident it is best not to handle opaque snakes.

Chapter Five: Breeding Kingsnakes

Copulating pair of Gray-banded Kingsnakes. Photo by Bob Applegate.

The successful breeding of kingsnakes is a culmination of all we have covered so far plus some. Breeding procedures for most kingsnakes can be described as almost a "recipe". The following procedures are the steps of this recipe.

HIBERNATION / BRUMATION

In the middle of October stop feeding adult breeders but maintain normal temperatures until November first. If you live in a temperate zone, beginning in November, turn off all lights and heat sources to lower the ambient room temperature to 50°F-55°F. In warmer climates a different approach could be used to get the desired 50°F-55°F room temperature. Some of the methods used may include air conditioners, fans on timers that allow cool night air to blow in, and finally the use of thermostatically controlled coolers used to maintain wines at the appropriate temperatures. The latter, though expensive, will allow one to cool snakes within closely controlled parameters at any time of the year. Because of the warm weather and high background temperatures of an area such as Southern California, it can sometimes take several weeks for the temperatures to drop to

Courtship in a pair of Honduran Milksnakes. An "albino" male and a normal-appearing female. Photo by Terry Dunham.

the desired level. This can cause problems with some of the montane species/subspecies, but does not seem to adversely affect the breeding of most kingsnakes. During this cooling period, keep the reptile room closed and try to keep temperature fluctuations to a minimum to avoid respiratory problems. Usually there should be no more than a ten degree variance over a two week period of time. Herpetoculturists refer to this cooling procedure as hibernation, although it is considered more accurate to call it "brumation", based on the most recent research. Most reptiles don't hibernate in the true sense because, even though their metabolism has slowed considerably, they can perform various levels of activity such as drinking and moving about.

However, the word brumation elicits associations that do not really fit from a herpetocultural point of view. Indeed, brumation has not been widely adopted by the herpetocultural community and will probably not be. It is a word that looks and sounds wrong. Doesn't the word "brumate" sound like something a cow should be doing out in the fields? The closest word to it in most people's memory is ruminate (not "brume", meaning winter from which it was derived). Brumate and brumation in terms of popular use simply do not work. It would make much more sense to expand the definitions of hibernation and hibernate to include the following:

hibernation: 1. a popular term used by herpetoculturists in reference to the winter cooling of amphibians and reptiles in captivity usually associated with reduced activity and fasting. 2. the process of being subjected to reduced winter temperatures and the associated reduced activity and fasting (used with amphibians and reptiles in the reference of herpetoculture).

to hibernate: 1. a popular term used by herpetoculturists in reference to establishing environmental conditions and exposing amphibians and reptiles to environmental conditions leading to hibernation. 2. a herpetocultural term meaning to undergo the process of hibernation with reference to amphibians and reptiles in captivity.

The above is a position that has been developed and adopted by both the author and the publisher. The terms hibernation and hibernate will be used in the rest of the text in reference to the above definitions.

Standard maintenance procedures during this cooling period consist of changing the water once a week, regularly cleaning up any defecations, checking for sheds and shedding problems, and recording anything of note.

RETURN TO NORMAL MAINTENANCE

On March 1, turn the heat/lights back on and provide temperature gradients that offer higher temperature areas, but have a background temperature of 80°F. Within one week start feeding and begin introducing and keeping pairs together at least one day per week for mating. Most of the kingsnakes will shed at least once, some twice, after hibernation before being ready to breed. A female ready to breed shortly after her first or second post hibernation shed has a scent which is often highly arousing to males ready to breed. Some of the subspecies routinely breed early in the season, some quite a bit later. Some individuals will breed at different times than is considered "normal" for the species/subspecies, so watch each snake carefully, even if you don't expect anything at that time. Sometimes you can feel or see developing ovarian follicles in a snake. To feel for these follicles let the snake crawl between your forefinger and thumb. Starting about mid-body, gently push your thumb up on the ventral surface until the ventral surface is pushed up into the ribcage. As she crawls (if you try to slide your hand she may tighten up her muscles and you won't be able to feel the follicles) over your thumb you may feel a succession of round "bumps" evenly spaced.

Hemipenes seen in copulating Honduran Milksnakes. Remember that snakes can be injured if disturbed while copulating. Photo by Bill Love.

They sometimes feel like those old "Pop Beads" jewelry. If these hard follicles are present you can safely suspect she is ready to breed, has just bred, or will be ready to do so very soon. A follicle is the part of the ovary where eggs develop. It breaks open and releases the egg to be fertilized at a later point in time. Be sure to have a male with her at this time.

Copulation times also vary greatly with the species/subspecies of kingsnakes. Some are "quickies" averaging 10 minutes, some go well over two hours. After they separate there is usually a drop of seminal fluid that drops off the male hemipenis as it is withdrawn from the female. This can be collected, thinned with saline solution if necessary (contact lens solution works) and viewed at 200 power under a microscope with a shaded field. You should see sperm swimming around. If you don't see sperm, you may want to try a

Honduran Milksnake laying eggs. Photo by Terry Dunham.

second male. Most female kingsnakes will accept multiple "lovers", so it doesn't hurt to introduce a second male and try again. You don't want to miss providing good sperm to a receptive female that has developed follicles, or you may end up with infertile eggs (slugs). But if you do use a second male the parentage could be in question as your first "sterile male" may have had a few sperm passed. Unless you need the male elsewhere, leave him with "his" females. The more matings over a period of time, the better your chances for a good clutch of eggs. In many kingsnakes, the male will bite the neck region or head of the female while copulating.

Try to leave the "male of record" with "his" females, or at least have him visit them for a day or two each week. There are theories that suggest the first matings may simulate follicle development, and later matings or retained sperm actually fertilize the eggs. Sperm can be retained by a female kingsnake which she can use to fertilize her eggs even one year later. However, there seems to be a relationship whereby the longer the period of time between copulation and egg laying, the greater the percentage of infertile eggs that will occur.

A typical egg-laying container for kingsnakes and milksnakes. Photo by Bob Ashley.

Preferably, there should be a fresh "batch" of sperm available for each new group of follicles to be fertilized.

When the female is visibly swollen with eggs (the rear third of her body becomes quite distended) and becomes opaque, record it (see Records) and remove all cage mates. Prepare and introduce an "egg laying box" which can be any type of container that is large enough to comfortably hold the female, but small enough for her to feel confined and secure. The egg laying box should have an access hole large enough for her to easily slip through. It should also be about half filled with loosely packed damp (not dripping) sphagnum moss. As a rule, female kingsnakes will select this specially designed container as the egg laying site. I have never had a kingsnake choose the water bowl over the egg laying box for egg laying, but just in case, you may want to remove the water bowl, or lower the water level to 1/8"-1/4" depth, just enough for a drink, to play it safe. Some breeders choose to remove the snake from her cage and place her in a special cage or 5 gallon bucket partially filled with damp moss and sealed by a secure lid (with holes for air exchange). After her "pre-egg laying" shed (see Feeding for the recommended food regimen during this time), record the date then wait 6-10 days (varies with the species/ subspecies) for the eggs to be laid. If you use an opaque plastic food storage container, you will be able to see the eggs through the container and won't have to keep disturbing the snake.

Once the eggs are laid, check the female for retained eggs. If all appears well (she appears healthy and still has good body weight) then offer her several smaller food items. Within three days, put the male back in with her and try for a second or third clutch of eggs. It is preferable during this time to avoid feeding a female a large food item because when a male starts chasing her around to breed with her, she may regurgitate. If the same volume of food is consumed during this time but in smaller portions (i.e., several fuzzy or just-weaned mice instead of larger mice), she will normally hold her food down. Also several small meals gives more digestive surface than one larger one, getting more energy back into the female. When double clutching or triple clutching a female, it is a good idea to try to use the same snake who fathered the first clutch so that there will be no doubt about which snake fathered subsequent clutches. Because of retained sperm and delayed fertilization there could be questions as to which snake actually fathered a particular clutch. I understand if there are multiple males there can be multiple fathers to one clutch.

This procedure of collecting the eggs and feeding can go on as long as the females are willing and able to produce eggs. Most subspecies of kingsnakes will produce two clutches of eggs in a season. The exception being some of the Mountain kingsnakes that live at altitudes where the warm season is shorter. Often they will only produce one clutch per year. One type of milk snake, the Pueblan milk snake, routinely produces three clutches in one season. By late summer (Aug.-Sept.), female kingsnakes have usually stopped producing eggs. It then becomes important to feed them enough so that they regain their prime weight prior to hibernation. Again, your records and the general condition and appearance of the snake will help you determine if you meet this goal. Don't overlook the males at this time. It is easy to miss a seasonal weight loss in the males as we don't pay as much attention to them. This brings us to mid-October where we start the cycle again!

You may not have to hibernate all kingsnakes, a slight winter cooling will work with some. The above methods have been used successfully with kingsnakes that are found from Canada to Central America. This schedule has been designed to coincide with the seasons in North America. For other parts of the world, keep them warm and feeding longer if necessary, to coincide with your seasons if you imported them. They will acclimate quickly to the new seasonal timeframe. If they are produced in your country we will assume they have already been acclimated to the your seasons.

AGE AND ITS RELATION TO BREEDING AND FECUNDITY: THE IMPORTANCE OF LONG TERM PLANNING

The average female kingsnake will stop producing viable eggs at about 10 years of age. If it is important for you to produce a consistent number of babies each year, you need to take this age factor into consideration in your long term planning. When your female is 6-7 years old you should hold back or buy a baby female to grow up as her replacement. Males will perform slightly longer than females, but 10 years is a good general rule with them as well. Remember this is an average over a large group of snakes, yes I have had both males and females continue to be reproductively active over 20 years. You should also hold back or buy male babies so there will always be young "studs" capable of servicing several females.

DIVERSIFYING YOUR GENE POOL

Every so often try to "trade out" or buy babies of known origin from other kingsnake breeders so you don't have to interbreed siblings or related stock. So far, in snake breeding, there are relatively few examples of the "inbreeding syndrome" (but there are some) associated with reduced vigor and genetic problems. However, the "pros" who are setting up the stud books for threatened and endangered species say it is important to have as much "founder stock" (animals traceable to their wild origin) as possible to prevent the problems associated with inbreeding. This is another good reason for maintaining careful records on the snakes that we keep and breed.

EGG INCUBATION

Hatching kingsnake eggs is simple. You need four things: Fertile eggs, proper incubation temperature, proper humidity, and proper ventilation. How you control these factors can be varied. The proper temperature range for incubating

A simple incubator for incubating snake eggs.

kingsnake eggs is 78°F-88°F with a preferable range of 82°F-85°F. If you are on the cooler side it will take longer for your eggs to hatch. If you incubate the eggs at too low of a temperature, the babies may take an unusually long time to hatch (if they hatch) and will usually be thin, undernourished, and will often fare very poorly. If you exceed the safe temperatures, you risk deformities (if they hatch) or death.

The eggs are also tolerant of a relatively wide range of humidity. As long as the incubating medium or substrate is noticeably moist, the eggs should be OK. You can find all sorts of research about measuring the amount of moisture needed by snake eggs. The nice thing is that a wide range of humidity levels will work. If the substrate your eggs are sitting in/on feels moist to you, as long as there isn't any visible liquid in contact with the eggs, it will probably work fine. Without any moisture, the eggs will dry up and die; with too much, they will either drown (such as when laid in the water bowl) or absorb so much liquid that they rupture.

Proper ventilation is easily controlled as well. As long as there is some air exchange, the eggs will live. Avoid placing large clutches of eggs in the bottom of a deep container or jar. As a result of the respiration of the developing embryos, carbon dioxide, in a container allowing no or little air flow, can build up to where it covers the eggs and the clutch will smother. A decaying incubating medium can also produce harmful gases. This is one cause for eggs that go near full

This homemade incubator will hold about 700 kingsnake eggs. Photo by Bob Applegate.

term to fail to hatch, even though there are fully developed young inside.

AN INCUBATING SYSTEM THAT WORKS

Put the eggs on top of 3/4" of moistened vermiculite in the bottom of a plastic container (such as butter or cottage cheese containers). If the eggs are freshly laid and moist, you can gently pull a few apart so they fit better in the container, but if they are stuck leave them as a clump. Do not cover the eggs with vermiculite. Place this container and 5-7 more egg containers inside a plastic storage box (sweater box) with ventilation holes around the middle of the sides. Add about 1/2 to 3/4 of an inch of water to the bottom of the box with the egg containers "floating". Put the storage box lid on and incubate at 82°F. Record the date of laying and the number of eggs laid and the female's ID on the side of the egg containers.

This incubating system works very well for me. The eggs will remain relatively dry, but water will be evaporating all around them. The water will also maintain the preferred incubating temperature so that there will be no drastic temperature changes. Every time the lid or door is opened, fresh air will be allowed in. To keep a constant

Hatchling snakes will slit the egg with an egg tooth to free themselves from the egg. Photo by Bob Applegate.

temperature there are inexpensive commercial incubators available, or a simple one can be made with an aquarium or polystyrene foam ice chest and an aquarium heater. Some snake rooms or cages will maintain the proper temperature ranges. Some gradual temperature changes will not hurt the eggs. The difficulty in describing how to incubate is complicated. One reader may be in a desert area with low natural humidity, another in a humid jungle area. You will have to "tweek" your application of the above to fit your particular requirements to get the proper balances.

WHAT ABOUT THE GOOD FERTILE EGGS?

As simple as it sounds, this is the part over which we have the least control. If you set up the eggs properly and two weeks later the eggs still look good, most of those should hatch. If they mold, discolor, or start sweating, they were probably destined to die, and there isn't a darned thing we can do about it.

INCUBATION PROBLEMS

There are times when a clutch of eggs incubates for over two months, then hatches, except for one or two eggs that have died and

A hatchling Gray-banded Kingsnake emerges from the egg. Photo by Bill Love.

completely rotted away. These eggs are usually in the center of the clutch and could not be safely removed. As a rule, don't be too worried about removing bad eggs during incubation. If they smell, sweat, discolor, and you can easily pull or separate them, then, by all means, do so. The incubator will smell better and it will help keep the air from going "stale." However, be careful not to ruin a good neighboring egg by rupturing its shell while trying to pry out a bad egg. Try to leave the eggs in the basic position they are found, relative to the top and bottom of the eggs.

CARRION FLIES

If you are unfortunate enough to have those nasty little humpbacked carrion flies attack your bad eggs, you will need to take action. If allowed to lay numerous eggs and to multiply in your incubator, they can and will kill good eggs, particularly those attached to bad ones. If present, you may have to actually wash the clutch in lukewarm fresh water. Use a soft brush to remove fly eggs, and change the egg substrate to rid yourself of these flies.

INCUBATING LARGE NUMBERS OF EGGS

When there are several clutches incubating, it is a good idea to stack the incubating boxes in sequence so the box containing the oldest eggs is always on the top. There it will be easier to watch for unexpected hatchlings. When a clutch is expected to hatch, the container with the clutch can be taken out of the plastic storage box and transferred into a smaller plastic shoe box. A very small amount of water should be added to the floor of the box and it should then be placed elsewhere in the incubator. This will allow you to keep exact records of how many snakes will have hatched in a given clutch (container) without the danger of them getting mixed up with others hatching at the same time inside the larger plastic storage box. Also, with larger hatchlings, I have had them hatch in the "community" container and try to burrow under another clutch of eggs, dumping them in the water.

RECOMMENDED PROCEDURES WITH HATCHING EGGS

Like most snakes, kingsnakes, following slitting of the egg shell, do not immediately emerge from the egg. Under no circumstance should you prematurely force a baby out of the egg. If it has slit the egg, let it stay in the egg for several days if it wants to. If forced out, a baby snake may rupture small blood vessels that are not ready to be separated from the egg remains, and bleed to death. If most eggs are slit (baby snakes cut the shell with their egg tooth) and a day or two later there are eggs that haven't slit, carefully slit the high point of the egg with cuticle scissors. Cut a 1" long slit, then a 1/4" cross cut at right angles to the center of the long cut, to be sure the baby can squeeze out. You don't want to lose a baby just because it lost an egg tooth or the shell is a little too thick.

Records

A very important and surprisingly useful aspect of herpetoculture is record keeping. Every snake should have an individual record card. Five inch by eight inch file cards have proven to be a convenient size. Each card should have the snake's sex, the common and scientific name, the source of origination, and a description of any distinguishing marks. Feeding and shedding data should also be

A data card for tracking feeding, shedding, and other information. Photo by Bob Applegate.

recorded on the card. This information can be stored in a relatively small space. The weight of each snake when hatched, along with before and after hibernation, can also be recorded on the card.

On the reverse side, record any disease/parasite problems and dates of treatment. For the males record dates of copulation, females copulated with, sperm check, and any other noteworthy observations. For females record copulation date and which male, sperm check results, date of egg laying, number of eggs that look "good," weight of the egg clutch, weight of the female, date and number of eggs hatching, and the sex ratio of the hatchlings. Add anything you might find interesting.

Some information on the cards is of general interest and can be referred to from time to time, but other information can be of a critical and timely nature. What is "critical" information? Which snakes need to be bred, which are due for their pre-egg laying shed (they might need help, you deffinitely do NOT want a shed problem now), and which cages have snakes due to lay eggs.

To keep track of which snakes need to be bred, make a diagram of your collection and place it above their cages. In each "cage" on the diagram put the sex and subspecies (example: Lth = *Lampropeltis triangulum hondurensis*). When mating is observed, circle the female and put a check under the male if good sperm is found. As the season progresses you can quickly glance at this diagram and spot any unmated female that may require special attention. Also, if a male is needed to fill in for a sterile one, a quick glance at the check marks under a male will make it easy to get a "good one".

Once the females have bred and are gravid, it then becomes important to know when they will lay eggs. To solve this dilemma, I use a wall-mounted chalk board. On it are drawn three columns of boxes. Fortunately, the kingsnakes can be depended upon to shed their skin a predetermined number of days before actually laying eggs. The number of days between the shed and the egg laying varies with the species/subspecies, but is fairly consistent within each. Eggs which are laid before or after the expected time are usually infertile or otherwise not going to hatch. If you observe an opaque snake that is gravid, put the cage number and her number in column one. When she sheds put that date in column two, remove any cage mates (yes, some kingsnakes will eat the fresh eggs of others of their kind), and place an egg-laying container in the cage. Column three is for the date and number of eggs laid. A glance at the board will tell which cages need to be checked for sheds or eggs. A second glance at the diagram will tell who "needs a boyfriend." Locate one and bring them together. All of this didn't require sorting through a single individual record card!

There are other variables worth recording which may prove to be valuable sources of information in the future. In addition to the above, I also record the ambient room temperatures, both highs and lows (use a high/low thermometer), on a two week cycle. This seemingly insignificant bit of information helped me solve persistent fertility problems in Arizona Mountain Kingsnakes (*Lampropeltis pyromelana*) and Durango Mountain Kingsnakes (*Lampropeltis mexicana greeri*).

With records such as these you can calculate your cost in mice in raising an individual snake, compare results with different management techniques, see results when comparing the breeding of different sized animals, determine the smallest sizes to safely breed (or hold back and grow one more season), growth rates, egg clutch

A beautiful example of the Pale Milk Snake, *L. t. multistriata*. Photo by Don Soderberg.

sizes, sex ratios on hatchlings, incubation times at various temperatures, etc. You can also formulate lots of graphs and charts to use for formal presentations. You may not use much of this information when things are routine and going well, but if there ever is a problem, this type of information will often help you or others determine what that problem is. Over time through the use of records, the trends of individual specimens will show up as different from others of their species/subspecies and will allow you to adapt your husbandry to their special needs. Remember, with nature all rules are general and there are often exceptions. I don't care what "the book says," snakes can't read. Expect exceptions.

If you are a professional snake breeder, there will also be other types of records that you will have to maintain such as those pesky business and IRS records, but the title of this book is NOT "How to Make a Million Bucks Raising Snakes." Those types of records should be established between you and your tax attorney.

Chapter SIX: Diseases and Disorders

Kingsnakes thrive in almost all "snake acceptable" habitats there are in the wild. That should give you a clue as to their adaptability as a species. If you meet their basic needs they will live a long healthy life. However, as with most life forms, there are certain problems to watch for.

Shedding Problems

Milk snakes seem to have comparatively thin skins. Shedding problems are very common and need to be monitored. These problems are covered in the "Shedding" section.

External Parasites

The most common external parasites are snake mites. They are tiny speck-sized blood sucking invertebrates or arachnids. The next most common external parasites in wild-caught animals are ticks. In many books there are detailed instructions on how to clean and sterilize the cage and its contents to eliminate mites. Some areas have mites on their wild populations of reptiles, and no matter how careful and clean you are, mites will find their way in.

The obvious first step in preventing mite infestations is prevention by quarantining any new snake in a separate room from where a collection is kept. During the quarantine period (3-4 weeks minimum is recommended) you will be able to assess the health status of your new snake including the presence of mites. Mites can be deterred and controlled by using a few commercially made products. One such product called "Provent A Mite®" can be used as a prophylactic as it can be used to create a barrier that mites will not cross. This product comes in an aerosol type can and can be sprayed on the cage furniture, the cage floor, and most importantly the cage vents and perimeter of the openings. This product is not meant to be sprayed on the snake directly. The snake enclosure should then be thoroughly wiped and disinfected with a 5% bleach solution as should any cage furnishings. Repeat the process in 2 weeks. Remember that when treating mites, if you miss a few eggs or one gravid mite, the problem will eventually return.

Ticks

Most ticks will be killed by using the same treatment as used for mites. The easiest way to contend with ticks, however, is to apply rubbing alcohol on the tick body using a cotton swab. After 5 to 10 minutes, the tick can easily be pulled off using round-nosed tweezers. Be sure to remove the tick's mouthparts when removing it from the snake.

Internal Parasites

Wild kingsnakes can harbor a multitude of internal parasites including worms and protozoa, some of which haven't been identified. Captive-hatched animals are usually clean (a lot depends on the husbandry of your breeder/supplier), but sometimes can be infested with worms.

A common parasite is the flagellate protozoan *Trichomonas* (those things you see crazily swimming around in random patterns when you are looking for the serpentine swimming motion of sperm). *Trichomonas* are easy to eliminate. Metronidazol (Flagyl-Searle Labs) can be safely administered orally at a dosage of 50 mg/kg (2.2 lbs.) to eliminate them. A fresh stool sample should be taken to a vet for analysis for new snakes or ones you suspect have internal parasites. Caution: Milk snakes can react negatively to higher doses of Metronidazol than can be tolerated by other snake and reptile species.

Treatment for worms includes the use of Panacur® (Fenbendazole) given orally at a dose of 100 mg/kg.

Other Internal Parasites

Herpetoculturally we live in exciting times. Our animals are a valuable commodity which the veterinary community has recognized. They have been, and are currently doing research into veterinary reptile care. In the "old days" we tried to treat our reptiles by ourselves. Failing to find a cure, we desperately took our almost dead snake to a veterinarian. If they would even look at it, he or she would disappear into the back room, pull a reference book off the shelf, thumb to the reptile chapter, and try to match the problem with one of the cures given. Usually we returned home with a dead snake and a vet bill that exceeded the value of the snake when it was healthy. Not so anymore!!

If you suspect internal parasites but can't identify them, you will need the help of a veterinarian, so let him or her suggest the latest and best treatment. If you are advanced enough to identify the problem, you will probably be informed on the latest treatment. An important reference book with regards to reptile parasites and diseases is *Reptile Care* by Frederic Frye (1991, T.F.H.). *Understanding Reptile Parasites* by Roger Kilingberg is an inexpensive, user-friendly book as well.

Mouth Rot / Stomatitis

This disease is not common in kingsnakes. The earliest symptoms are small reddish spots along the gum line often accompanied with some excess mucus. In time, particularly if the snake is stressed, these symptoms may develop into full fledged mouth rot with the accompanying accumulations of whitish "cheesy" matter along the gum and teeth line. Without opening the mouth, one sign of this disease is when a snake's mouth just doesn't close right, leaving a small, barely visible asymmetrical gap between the two jaws. Untreated this infection will ultimately affect the bone and kill the snake. Fortunately it is easily treated when recognized early on. Daily applications of hydrogen peroxide, Listerine®, or Neosporin® with a cotton swab will clear the infection within a week or two. If severe, with the teeth line extensively affected, a veterinarian should be consulted to administer antibiotics in addition to the topical therapy. Snakes infected with mouth rot should be isolated from other specimens until they are healed.

Respiratory Infections

In general, kingsnakes are very resistant to respiratory infections. However, if they are stressed they may sometimes come down with symptoms of a respiratory infection including "blowing bubbles", inactivity, refusing to feed, gaping, forced exhalations and/or excess mucus in the mouth. Examples of stress-causing situations are not enough nutrition (depletion) after egg laying, excessive fluctuations in temperature, too cool temperatures, and/or poor sanitary conditions.

With time, these stresses can lead to mouth-rot (infectious stomatitis) or pneumonia. If noticed early and if the associated environmental or maintenance factors are corrected you may reverse the course of the infection by simply raising the temperature in the cage to 88°F-90°F until the snake's health improves. When snakes are sick they often seek heat. The immune system of the snake will also function better at higher temperatures, and it may allow it to "cure" itself.

If, after a few days at higher temperatures, you don't notice an improvement, or if the disease has progressed to pneumonia (gaping and forced exhalation are indicative symptoms), you will probably need a veterinarian to administer antibiotics to save your snake. Sometimes respiratory problems can be caused by parasitic worms burrowing through the lungs (primarily in wild-caught animals). Respiratory diseases can also result from allergic reactions to a substrate of if a cage is not properly maintained, to ammonia gas released by moist waste. Veterinarians spend years in school to learn this stuff, and read and study constantly (the ones I want you to go to do). If you provide proper husbandry for the kingsnake and one of your snakes develops a problem you can't easily recognize and fix—SEE A VETERINARIAN!!

Egg Impaction

Sometimes kingsnakes, particularly those laying large clutches of eggs, will not be able to pass the last few eggs. Various theories suggest calcium deficiencies and inactivity leading to muscle weakness (the snake is so tired and weak it can't find the strength to lay the last couple of eggs). It seems this muscle weakness is a major problem because when many of the "stuck" eggs are removed they are no larger than those already passed. However, lets face it, our snakes are lazy! They don't do nearly the work in our cages that they do in the wild, so it's easy to see how their muscles would become weak. But what can we do? Run our snakes around the house or yard daily? Take them to one of Gary Larson's snake gyms? The problem is being researched, and hopefully an answer will be forthcoming, but if you find out first, please let me know. We don't have the answer yet.

However, when eggs become impacted there are several things that can be done. If there is an egg near the vent it can be gently palpated out. If the egg is too large, exert some pressure and when the tail lifts, and you see the end of the egg or find the entry to the oviduct (up against the backbone), you can puncture and drain the egg using a large syringe and needle. If there are more eggs "up high," give them a few days to work their way down to the vent. If they fail to "come down", insert a blunt well-lubricated instrument up into the oviduct and try to work the end first to, then past the next egg. Apply gentle pressure on the egg and, leaving the instrument in position as a guide, try to palpate the egg along the instrument down to the vent where it can be forced out or removed by puncturing the shell and pulling it out. The instrument keeps the oviduct from turning. If the oviduct is allowed to turn it can be "prolapsed" and be forced out with the egg, tearing it loose and severely damaging the snake. Another technique is to try to drain the contents from the egg through the outer body wall, using a large gauge needle passed between the ribs. With the reduced size, the eggs may pass. This procedure could contaminate the oviduct with "spilled" egg contents and lead to infection, but it has worked for many, and the patient has gone on to successfully breed the next season. Sometimes, just handling the snake and making it move around may help dislodge the "stuck" eggs. In other cases, veterinary surgery may be required. As should be apparent from the above techniques, it is highly recommended that anyone inexperienced with procedures relating to egg impaction should consult an experienced herpetological veterinarian. This could make the difference between life and death.

Final Comments

This beautiful Ruthven's Kingsnake was photographed in its natural habitat in Michoacan, Mexico. Photo by Jeff Lemm.

What is our world coming to? We have government agencies on local, state and federal levels telling us (or trying to) what we can and can't do with our animals. Their efforts to save the animals "for future generations" need help. Aren't we part of that government? It seems like I remember something from school about "government of the people, by the people, and for the people." What happened to that philosophy? Does this mean that if most people don't like snakes then they should be against the law? With all the emphasis on minority rights these days I don't see how that can possibly be. So what can we do?

Don't you just love it when someone receiving salaries from tax dollars (your money) advises other "officials" who receive their salaries from tax dollars or fishing and hunting license fees (your money), that the "private person" (you, who pays their salaries) should not be allowed to sell "native reptiles" for a profit, even if they are captive produced? Are we going to be so stupid as to wait until animals we want are almost extinct or unavailable from the wild

Prairie Kingsnake, *Lampropeltis calligaster*. Photo by Bob Applegate.

before we bring the last few into captivity to save them? The California Condor is a good example. Look at the public (you and me) money being spent to bring the last few into captivity and breed them in captivity (their only chance) to keep this great bird from going into extinction. If, 50 years ago, these birds had been allowed to be kept and bred we would still have enough to supplement the wild populations from captive-bred stock and the emergency, last-ditch-chance mentality wouldn't exist now. It's the same story with some of the hoofed mammals being captive-bred and released into the wild. We should be allowed to take wild stock (in limited numbers that wild populations could lose and still be viable), breed them, and sell the babies. We would pay our taxes on the profit. Those taxes wouldn't have to be spent later to finance "conservation through propagation" projects initiated by "officials" at great cost to us. There would be a genetic pool of many species in captivity available to supplement wild populations. We, the herpetologically oriented public may not be able to captive breed endangered elephants or rhinos, but most reptiles are perfect for the private domain.

How do we accomplish this? Organize!! We have to convince the majority that although they may not like what we do, we are harmless to them, and we have a right to exist and to do what we are doing. How can we organize? I wish I knew! There are so many reptile people now that are illegal where they live, that they don't dare expose themselves for fear of arrest and confiscation of their animals.

Should we be allowed to keep venomous? Of course, if we are deemed responsible and liable for any damages or injuries that might occur. Without a legal way to keep these venomous, people will do so anyway, but underground, and when found out, yet another set of bad laws will be enacted. There are enough "dangerous nusiance" laws on the books to cover public encounters with reptiles, we don't need specific reptile bans. Join your local herpetological society for regional affairs and information. There is power in numbers. Thanks for letting me vent here, now get out there and accomplish something!

And lastly, I would like to make an appeal for cooperation between the scientific and private herpetologist/herpetoculturist communities. Yes, I know we don't trust each other, and there are and have been good reasons on both sides. But we both have information useful to the other side. Wouldn't it be a perfect world if the herpetologists acquire a new species, but instead of preserving it, turn it over to a captive breeder? The breeder "makes more" of them so the scientist can see if the original scalation, patterns, etc., described hold true for a larger sample, and there are now more available to all to enjoy and/or study. We all get to learn the habits and requirements of living specimens. When the wild caught founder stock dies, it is then preserved and sent into a study collection. Trust has to be earned on both sides, but the results should be worth the efforts."

Thanks to some hard work and luck of some private individuals, here is the first published photo of a living *Lampropeltis webbi*. This adult female is from El Palmito, Sinaloa, Mexico. Photo by Paul Lynuma, Chris Grunwald and Jason Jones.

SINALOAN MOUNTAIN KINGSNAKE
Lampropeltis webbi

Describing the individual species is beyond the scope intended for this book, but there has been a new species of kingsnake just described in 2005 and many will be hearing about it for the first time here, and will see a picture of a living specimen for the first time so I will pass along some information about the snake that has been provided to me.

The Sinaloan Mountain Kingsnake (*Lampropeltis webbi*). The Holotype (The first specimen the description was based on), UANL 5684, was first found in June of 2000 by Dr. Robert Bryson. Paratype(a second specimen) FWMSH 6716) was later found unidentified in a preserved collection. It was collected in August 1968 by W.J. Voss. The snake was named after Dr. Robert Webb for his years of herpetological work in NW Mexico.

Natural habitat of *Lampropeltis webbi*. Photo by Paul Lynuma, Chris Grunwald, and Anish Yeleker.

As of now, *webbi* is only known from the Pacific side of the Sierra Madre Occidental in the Mexican state of Sinaloa. All known specimens have been found on and near Hwy. 40 near the Sinaloa and Durango state lines.

It is expected that further research will extend the range into Durango as well as Nyarit. Specimens have been collected during the day in rocky outcrops in open tropical pine covered hillsides. Specimens found on the road have been discovered on steep, rocky, densely vegetated oak-and pine-covered hillsides. Specimens field-collected during the day were in July as the monsoon season had just started. After the ground had received enough moisture, usually by August, all specimens were found on Hwy. 40 at night during the height of the monsoon season. Several of these snakes were collected in the 1960s and 1970s, most were mis-identified and/or lost.

Luckily a few herpers felt they had something new, kept a few and are now working with them in captivity. Hopefully some will become available to all. As far as I know, the only ones known to the scientists are the two dead preserved specimens.

This found-on-road dead and preserved and one other preserved specimen are what are known to science and described as a new species. Photo by Dr. Devon Hartmann.

A very special thanks to Paul Lynum, Anish Yeleker, Chris Grunwald, Dr. Robert Bryson, Dr. Devon Hartmann, and Jason Jones for this otherwise unavailable information.

PHOTO GALLERY

Durango Mountain Kingsnake, *Lampropeltis mexicana greeri.* Photo by Don Soderberg.

Hypomelanistic Durango Mountain Kingsnake, *Lampropeltis mexicana greeri.* Photo by Bob Applegate.

An unusually patterned California Kingsnake, *Lampropeltis getula californiae*. Photo by Jill Griffith.

Lavender California Kingsnake, *Lampropeltis getula californiae*. Photo by Don Shores.

Kingsnakes and Milksnakes

A New Mexico Milksnake, *Lampropeltis triangulum celaenops*. Photo by Bob Applegate.

Ruthven's Kingsnake, *Lampropeltis ruthveni*. Photo by Bob Applegate.

Normal Speckled Kingsnake, *Lampropeltis getula holbrooki*. Photo by Bill Love.

Albino Speckled Kingsnake, *Lampropeltis getula holbrooki*. Photo by Bob Applegate.

An unusual speckled Mexican Gray-banded/San Luis Potosi Kingsnake, *Lampropeltis mexicana*. Photo by Don Shores.

A Gray-banded Kingsnake, *Lampropeltis alterna*. Photo by Don Soderberg.

Arizona Mountain Kingsnake, *Lampropeltis pyromelana*. Photo by Don Soderberg.

Hypomelanistic Arizona Mountain Kingsnake, *Lampropeltis pyromelana*. Photo by Bob Applegate.

Kingsnakes and Milksnakes

An albino Eastern Milksnake, *Lampropeltis triangulum triangulum*. Photo by Bill Love.

Hypomelanistic tricolor Honduran Milksnake, *Lampropeltis triangulum hondurensis*. Photo by Don Shores.

A bi-colored Honduran Milksnake, *Lampropeltis triangulum hondurensis*. Photo by Don Shores.

Snow Honduran Milksnake. Photo by Terry Dunham.

Two phases of the Apalachicola Kingsnake, *Lampropeltis getula goini*. Photo by Bob Applegate.

Axanthic Brooks' Kingsnake, *Lampropeltis getula brooksi*. Photo by Don Shores.

Brooks' Kingsnake, *Lampropeltis getula brooksi*. Photo by Don Soderberg.

A beautiful hypomelanistic Brooks' Kingsnake, *Lampropeltis getula brooksi*. Photo by Don Soderberg.

A gorgeous Pueblan Milksnake. Photo by Don Shores.

An albino motley Nelson's Milksnake, *Lampropeltis triangulum nelsoni*. Photo by Don Shores.

How are some of these strange patterns created in captivity?

First you have to find, from normal patterned stock, something you want to try to duplicate such as combining the albino and striped phase Sinaloan Milksnake. After 2-3 generations and several years, you prove they are both recessive traits and try to combine them.

When the clutch hatches, you have a group of normal colored babies, but if your calculations are correct, they are all carrying recessive genes for both albino and striped patterns. Spend another few years growing these up and breed them together.

Kingsnakes and Milksnakes

These clutches will hatch out with quite a mix but there will be four basic combinations: Some are normal looking, some are striped, some are albino . . .

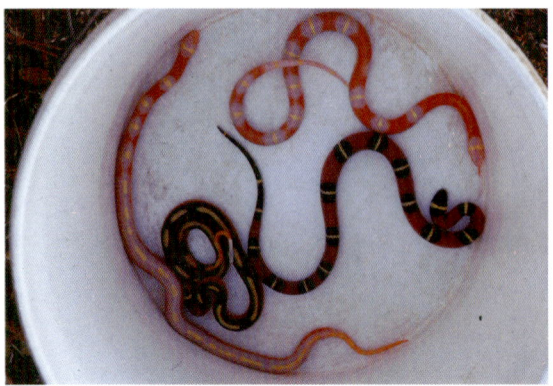

. . . and with any luck at all, one out of 16 should be the "Rainbow" or Albino Striped Sinaloan Milksnake.

. . . and the project only took about 12 years to complete!

SUGGESTED READING

Anonymous. 1994. Maintainance and breeding of the Honduran milksnake *Lampropeltis triangulum hondurensis* at Edinburgh Zoo. Scottish Herpetological Society Newsletter. 1994 (December):1-4.

Applegate, Robert W. 1988. The Pueblan milksnake (*Lampropeltis triangulum campbelli*): a case for captive propagation. Vivarium. 1 (2):49-53.

Assetto, Robert Jr. 1978. Reproduction in the Gray-Banded Kingsnake, *Lampropeltis mexicana alterna*. Herp. Rev, 9:56-57

Bartlett, R. D. 1994. Kingsnakes of Florida. Tropical Fish Hobbyist. 42 (10):116-126.

Blanchard, Frank N. 1919. Two new snakes of the genus *Lampropeltis*. Occasional Papers of the Museum of Zoology, University of Michigan. (70):1-11.

Blanchard, Frank N. 1920. Three new snakes of the genus *Lampropeltis*. Occasional Papers of the Museum of Zoology, University of Michigan. (81):1-10.

Blaney, R. M. 1977. Systematics of the Common Kingsnakes, *Lampropeltis getulus*, Tulane Studies in Zoology and Botany.

Blaney, R. M. 1979. The status of the outer banks kingsnake, *Lampropeltis getulus sticticeps* (Reptilia: Serpentes: Colubridae). Brimleyana. 1 125-128.

Conant, Roger and Joseph T. Collins. 1998. Reptiles and Amphibians of Eastern and Central North America: 3rd Edition, Houghton Mifflin Press, Boston.

Condit, John M. and Robert E. Woodruff. 1955. An albino milksnake, *Lampropeltis doliata triangulum*, from Ohio. Copeia. 1955 (3):257.

Cranston, Thurgess. 1991. Notes on the Natural History, Husbandry, and Breeding of the Gray-Banded Kingsnake, *Lampropeltis alterna*. The Vivarium, 3(2):7-10

Cranston, Thurgess. 1997. Natural history and captive husbandry of the Mexican Milk Snake, *Lampropeltis triangulum annulata*. The Vivarium. 8 (5):48-50;68.

Dunham, Terry. 1996. Marvelous mutants: Honduran milksnakes. Reptilian. 4 (7):36-37.

Frye, F. 1991. Biomedical and Surgical Aspects of Captive Reptile Husbandry. Krieger Publishing. pp. 712.

Gehlbach, Frederick R. and Ronald K. Baker. 1962. Kingsnakes Allied with *Lampropeltis mexicana*: Taxonomy and Natural History, Copeia 1962 #2

Gillingham, J. C., C. C. Carpenter, B. J. Bruce and J. B. Murphy. 1977. Courtship and copulatory behavior of the mexican milksnake, *Lampropeltis triangulum sinaloe* (Colubridae). The Southwestern Naturalist. 22 (2):187-194.

Greene, Harry W. 1979. Systematics and natural history of the American milksnake, *Lampropeltis triangulum*. Copeia. 1979 (1):180-181.

Groves, John D. and Robert J. Assetto. 1976. *Lampropeltis triangulum elapsoides*. Herpetological Review. 7 (3):114.

Hammack, Stephen H. 1993. History & Captive propagation of the Andean milk snake (*Lampropeltis triangulum andesiana*). Captive Breeding. 1 (4):17-19;22-24.

Herman, Dennis W. 1979. Captive reproduction in the scarlet kingsnake, *Lampropeltis triangulum elapsoides* (Holbrook). Herpetological Review. 10 (4):115.

Kardon, Alan and Erik R. Holmback. 1996. Husbandry and reproduction of the giant Central American black milksnake *Lampropeltis triangulum gaigeae*. Vivarium. 7 (4):14-16.

Klingenberg, R. 1997. Understanding Reptile Parasites. Advanced Vivarium Systems. Lakeside, CA.

Lewke, Robert E. 1979. Neck-biting and other aspects of reproductive biology of the Yuma kingsnake (*Lampropeltis getulus*). Herpetologica. 35 (2):154-157.

Lowe, Dave. 1997. Keeping and breeding common kingsnakes (*Lampropeltis getulus* and its various subsepecies). The Herptile. 22 (1):26-37.

Mara, W. P. 1995. The Sinaloan milk snake. Reptile Hobbyist. 1 (2):36-42.

Markel, Ronald G. 1990. Kingsnakes and Milk Snakes. TFH Publications, Neptune, NJ.

Merker, Gerold and Walter Merker. 2005. Alterna: The Gray-Banded Kingsnake.

Mulks, Mitchell and Gerold Merker. 2004. Zonata: The California Mountain Kingsnake.

Nolan, Mike. 1994. Notes on the care and captive breeding of the Sinaloan milk snake (*Lampropeltis triangulum sinaloae*). pp. 93-98. *In* Simon Townson (eds.) Breeding Reptiles & Amphibians. British Herpetological Society, London.

Peterson, Karl H., David Lazcano and Ramiro D. Jacobo Galván. 1995. Captive reproduction in the Mexican milksnake *Lampropeltis triangulum annulata*. Litteratura Serpentium. 15 (5):128-132.

Secor, Stephen M. 1987. Courtship and mating behavior of the speckled kingsnake, *Lampropeltis getulus holbrooki*. Herpetologica. 43 (1):15-28

Stebbins, Robert C. 1985. Western Reptiles and Amphibians, 2nd Edition, Houghton Mifflin Press, Boston.

Tanner, Wilmer W. 1953. A Study of Taxonomy and Phylogeny of *Lampropeltis pyromelana* Cope. Great Basin Natur. 13(1-2): 47-66.

Tanner, Wilmer W. and Douglas Cox. 1981. Reprouction in the Snake *Lampropeltis pyromelana*. Great Basin Natur. 41(3): 314-316.

van het Meer, Jan. 1996. The care, maintenance, and breeding of *Lampropeltis getulus californiae* (Blainville, 1835). Litteratura Serpentium. 16 (1):14-17.

Williams, Kenneth L. 1978. Systematics and Natural History of the American Milk Snake, *Lampropeltis triangulum*. Milwaukee Public Museum, Milwaukee, WI.

Williamson, Michael A. 1972. *Lampropeltis triangulum celaenops*. Herpetological Review. 4 (5):170.

Wilson, Larry D. and Meyer, John R. 1985. The Snakes of Honduras: 2nd Edition, Milwaukee Museum Press.

Winstel, Al. 1991. Captive Husbandry of the eastern milk snake (*Lampropeltis t. triangulum*). Vivarium. 2 (6):16-17;28.

Zweifel, R. G. 1952. Pattern variation and evolution of the Mountain Kingsnake, *Lampropeltis zonata*. Copeia. 1952 (3):152-168.

Zweifel, R. G. 1981. Genetics of color pattern polymorphism in the California kingsnake. Journal of Heredity. 72 238-244.

ECO WEAR & Publishing

Celebrate the awe-inspiring diversity of wildlife in our natural world!

http://www.reptileshirts.com   517-487-5595